# CANADIAN LEGISLATIVE BEHAVIOR

A Study of the 25th Parliament

# CANADIAN LEGISLATIVE BEHAVIOR

## A Study of the 25th Parliament

ALLAN KORNBERG

Duke University

HOLT, RINEHART AND WINSTON

New York Chicago San Francisco Atlanta Dallas
Montreal Toronto London

Library of Congress Catalog Card Number: 67-26163

2654309

Printed in the United States of America

1 2 3 4 5 6 7 8 9

# PREFACE

This is a book about legislative behavior in a Canadian House of Commons. In the analysis of this institution I have used the concepts of role and reference group and the method of survey research that in the past have been employed with great success in research on American legislators.

Most of the data used were derived from structured interviews with Canadian Members of Parliament (MPs). The assumption that underlies the collection, organization, and analysis of the data is that legislative behavior is a product of the interaction between the individual legislator, the influence of his society, and the legislative institution per se. The behavior of the legislator has been conceptualized as a series of roles determined by the values and attitudes he brings to the legislative position and by the perspectives he develops as an incumbent. Since subcultural influences are assumed to affect his values and attitudes, I have tried to delineate the political and cultural environment in which a Canadian MP grows up, his motives for entering into political activity, and the circumstances surrounding his recruitment as a candidate for Parliament. Because institutions and processes are assumed to influence behavior, I have analyzed the essential features of the Canadian parliamentary system within a framework of properties and attributes common to all democratic legislative bodies. Finally, since the perspectives he develops after incumbency also are important, I have described his goals, his motives for sustaining a parliamentary career, his attitudes toward constituents and party, and the manner in which he is likely to behave in the event of conflict between these institutions and his own predispositions.

All research is comparative, at least implicitly. However, I have attempted to be explicit in my comparisons, most often with findings from American studies in this area. Like John Wahlke, Heinz Eulau, Leroy Ferguson, and William Buchanan, the authors of *The Legislative System,* I want to delineate certain legislative roles. I have also tried to explain variations in roles taken and the relationships between these roles and other aspects of legislative behavior. If I have been successful to any degree, it is a result of the stimulation provided by Wahlke, Eulau, Ferguson, and Buchanan as well as by other scholars in the field of legislative behavior.

Apart from any contribution this study may make to the analytic subfield of legislative behavior, I hope a quantitative and empirical study will encourage further systematic research in Canadian politics. I am also concerned with the bicultural aspect of Canadian society. Thus, considerable attention has been given to an examination of the assumption that French Canadians and their legislative representatives differ significantly in attitude and behavior from their English and English-oriented countrymen.

In Chapter 1 legislative attributes and behavior are discussed in very general terms. In Chapter 2 the focus is on the attributes and behavior manifested in the Canadian parliamentary system.

Chapter 3 compares the respondents' social backgrounds with those of American Congressmen and candidates for the British House of Commons. The process by which Canadian MPs become interested in politics and initially are recruited for political activity also is examined. The section is concluded with a description of the legislators' preparliamentary careers and their future political aspirations.

Chapter 4 is a delineation of the circumstances surrounding the legislators' candidacies; specifically, it deals with the positions they held at the time of their nominations, whether or not the nominations were contested, and their motives for becoming candidates for Parliament. A discussion of the goals of Canadian MPs concludes this chapter.

In Chapter 5 we test our theoretical notion that the behavior of legislators is a product of expectations for the position derived from experiences prior to incumbency and attitudes and perspectives developed subsequently. This is done by analyzing the associations between variations in legislators' goals and selected prior and post incumbency variables. An alternative theory, termed an extreme culturalist theory of legislative behavior, is also tested with the data. The legislators' goals are then used as an independent variable to ascertain whether goal variations are associated with differences in other aspects of behavior.

In Chapter 6 the respondents' representational role orientations are delineated and compared with the orientations of American legislators at the national and state levels. The alternative theories of legislative behavior are tested and the relationships between representational role orientations and other aspects of legislative behavior are depicted.

Chapter 7 examines the Canadian legislative parties in terms of their normativeness, that is, the degree of control they exercise over individual MPs. The chapter attempts to determine whether shared attitudes toward policy issues and the opportunities provided by the party caucuses contribute to cohesive behavior. Chapter 8 presents the conclusions.

I learned a great deal about French Canada and its legislative representatives during conversations with certain French-Canadian professionals and during off-the-record discussions with individual French-Canadian MPs. I am indebted to Professor Samuel C. Patterson of the University of Iowa and to Professor William E. Wright of the University of Georgia who read this manuscript in its entirety and made numerous suggestions.

For permission to use portions of material previously published in several journals, I wish to thank the *American Political Science Review, The Journal of Politics, The Western Political Quarterly, Political Science, Parliamentary Affairs,* and *The Australian Journal of Politics and History.*

In the preparation of the manuscript Mrs. Frank Bean contributed her considerable skills as a typist.

Finally, the constant encouragement and enthusiam provided by my wife, Linda, has been an inspiration.

*Allan Kornberg*

DURHAM, NORTH CAROLINA
FEBRUARY 1967

# CONTENTS

# 1

# Legislatures

> Now any member of the Assembly, taken separately, is certainly inferior to the wise man. But the state is made up of many individuals . . . so a multitude is a better judge of many things than any one individual.
>
> *Aristotle*[1]

Legislatures are rather special types of institutions that carry out a variety of complex activities including making policies in the form of laws, criticizing and checking executive powers, and establishing administrative agencies whose duties are to implement the decisions which the legislature, as a body, has made. As the quotation from Aristotle indicates, legislatures long antedated the establishment of modern democratic institutions although historically they have been intimately associated with such institutions and practices. As recently as the Elizabethan era in England, the House of Commons was little more than a group of loyal supplicants gathered together to petition the Monarch on behalf of some local interest. The impact of the English, American, French, and Industrial revolutions, combined with the broad extension of the franchise in the nineteenth century, produced the modern democratic legislature. Today, legislatures are so apportioned that they represent their public psychologically and sometimes even physically. Through such mechanisms as political parties, interest groups, and elections, they are ultimately accountable to the societies of which they are a part. Yet, at the same time, the generally moderate level of political interest that the people in these societies display permits legislators a substantial degree of discretion in carrying out their functions.

Legislatures vary in the names by which they are commonly called, and so we speak of congresses, assemblies, and parliaments. This is a study of one such parliament, the Canadian House of Commons. The study was carried out in 1962, and the data that are presented were derived almost entirely from structured interviews with a stratified random sample of Canadian legislators. Of an ascribed sample of 171 members of Parliament (MPs), 166 interviews were taken; 165 of these interviews were used in preparing the present analysis. This is one of the few instances in which survey research methods have been employed in a study of the dynamics underlying the operation of a national legislature in a major Western democracy.[2]

There are three reasons for studying the Canadian or any other legislative body.[3] First, the generic function of a legislature is to make the values, goals, and attitudes of a social system authoritative in the form of legislative decisions.[4] When we study the decisions of a legislature, therefore, we are also, in a sense, studying the value patterns of the society in which it is a subsystem.

Second, legislators themselves provide cues and serve as reference groups for the behavior of their public. This is sometimes called the "educative function" of the legislature. Talcott Parsons[5] feels that education is one way in which decision-makers obtain the generalized support they seek in return for the leadership they provide and the binding decisions they make.

Third, legislatures often perform the function of facilitating a catharsis of societal grievances by providing a forum for their expression. Such a function frequently provides a valuable index for the analysis of a particular society. In a way, it is simpler to study the behavior of legislators than of the mass public not only because there are fewer subjects to focus upon, but also because legislatures are organizations and not merely agglomerations of individuals.

## COMMON ATTRIBUTES

The patterns of behavior of legislative bodies are characterized by certain regularities and uniformities.[6] Although the subject matter with which they deal changes, the manner in which they deal with it, with certain variations, is continually repeated. There are, then, certain properties that are common to all legislatures. Four such attributes deserving particular comment are recruitment, communication, structure, and normativeness.

## RECRUITMENT

Any legislative system, to remain viable, must establish and institutionalize mechanisms for the recruitment and selection of personnel. So fundamental is recruitment that both the process itself and the qualifications for prospective recruits are generally incorporated into the formal constitutional arrangements. Although it need not always be the case, an integral part of the recruitment process in democratic polities is the electoral system. Recruitment also involves such factors as apportionment, districting, the number of competing parties, and the quality of intraparty and interparty competition. Only selected aspects of the process are dealt with in this study.

## COMMUNICATION

And in the beginning, there was communication. This is very nearly so, if one accepts Norbert Weiner's[7] assumption that communication is the cement that makes organizations and holds them together, or that it alone enables any group to think, see, and act cohesively. In any legislature, communication makes possible the sharing of group-relevant attitudes, values, and norms that presuppose consensus and cohesion. In addition, interpersonal relationships are made stable and relatively predictable; the legislature, as an organization, is able to achieve the goals and perform the functions for which it was established.

Both the volume and the content of communication in any legislature are affected by its size and structure as well as by situational factors such as the number of parties and the prevailing informal behavioral norms. A large, single communication net based on face-to-face encounters is more likely to be found in small rather than large legislatures and in unicameral rather than bicameral organizations. Similarly, if the political situation necessitates building interparty coalitions, as was the case in the French Chamber of Deputies of the Third and Fourth Republics, the volume of communication between individuals in different parties is likely to be greater than in legislatures where such arrangements are unnecessary. Where prevailing informal norms prescribe an extensive range of nonpartisan interactions, as in the American Senate, there is also likely to be a greater volume of communications. There probably will also be a qualitative difference between communications there and communications in a legislature such as the British House of Commons.

## STRUCTURE

Another property common to all legislatures is that the behavior of individual members and the pattern of interaction among them are formally prescribed, most frequently, in written or unwritten constitutions. Legislatures may consist of one or two chambers. The legislative and executive powers may be fused in a cabinet committee, or they may be separated. The chief executive officer may be a president or a prime minister.

Even at the national level, legislatures vary in size; the New Zealand Parliament comprises eighty members, while the British House of Commons comprises 637 members. Obviously, the size of a legislature has an important effect on its operations and procedures. For example, the resources available for solving complex problems are partially a function of size. The larger the number of legislators, the more substantial the probability that some of them will possess certain specialized skills and aptitudes required for solving difficult problems. The likelihood is increased by the fact that Western legislative bodies generally are not recruited from a cross section of the population in which the several social classes are approximately equally represented, but from a society's upper socioeconomic (as measured by education and occupation) stratum. Better solutions for complex problems should, therefore, occur more frequently in larger rather than in smaller legislatures.

Large size, although it makes available more human resources, tends to have a deletorious effect upon the satisfaction of individual social-psychological needs. These needs stem, in no small part, from satisfactory participation in group activities. Since the actions of legislatures are oriented toward the achievement of particular goals within reasonable time limits, the more individuals who participate in the requisite deliberations and activities, the longer the time required to realize those goals. Generally, the more members there are in a legislature, the less will be their chances for even partial participation in activities. Aside from affecting group morale, large size also may affect the group unity of a legislature, as size limits the number of person-to-person interactions. Normally, in a larger legislative body, there is less opportunity for such interaction or for the formation of a network of close interpersonal relationships. However, all three effects of relative size can be mediated by two structural properties—specialization and integration.

### *Specialization*

Legislatures are characterized by varying degrees of specialization, as are all formal organizations. To a lesser or greater extent all are organized into committees which may range in size from a large number of highly specialized committees, such as exist in the American Congress, to the relatively few but wide-ranging "alphabet" committees of the British House of Commons. Through specialization, the debilitating effects of large size on individual morale and group unity can be vitiated while its benefits, in terms of available resources, can be retained.

### *Integration*

Integration, which is concerned with the relation of the different parts to the whole, also serves to mitigate the results of relative size. The degree to which the behavior of component parts is coordinated with the whole, and the relative independence of the one from the other varies with each legislature. In some legislatures, powerful committees (such as the Finance Committee in the French Chamber of Deputies during the Fourth Republic) or even subcommittees (for example, the late Senator McCarthy's investigating committee) may operate as virtually autonomous and independent units. In others, however, committees are very much the creatures of the legislature as a whole.

Parliamentary systems modeled on the British system have an additional integrating task in that they are required to mesh the executive functions with the legislative functions. The task is accomplished either by the majority party or by the coalition of parties from which the executive is drawn. As well as performing an integrative function, legislative parties (or factions in the case of one-party legislatures) also generate much of the conflict characteristic of democratic legislative bodies.

Although legislators engage in cooperative behavior to the extent that they share goals such as a desire to maintain the system and to enact legislation, conflict virtually is built into the decision process in all democratic legislatures in that both formal and informal processes exist for more than one individual, group, or party to realize their goals. Thus, the legislative process frequently has been depicted as a kind of continuous struggle among individual and groups of legislators.[8] Conflict, if left unchecked, will eventually threaten the continued viability of any organization. All legislatures, therefore, also exercise some degree of control over the behavior of their members.

## NORMATIVENESS

The degree of power that any group exerts over its members by reason of its norms may be referred to as normativeness.[9] Norms may be either formal or informal; both set forth the expectations the group has for its members or define appropriate and inappropriate behavior. The constitutional framework, judicial decision, fundamental legislative enactments, and the procedures through which the collective substantive powers of a legislative body are carried out may all serve to formally limit the range of behavior of the members. Informal norms, in addition to performing this function,[10] also may help to re-enforce obedience to formal rules.[11]

In order for legislative norms to be observed, they first must be "visible," that is, the legislators must recognize and know that others recognize their existence. Second, there must be sufficient latitude involved in the application of norms so that they are acceptable to a majority of members at any one time. Third, there must be available some effective sanction system (in the sense that it is perceived as detrimental or punitive) to enforce adherence to norms.

Although a sanction system is an important aspect of normativeness in that it helps secure members' compliance to rules, adherence to any rules on a regular basis is most apt to occur if the rules are voluntarily or self-enforced. Where this is the case, a legislature, party, faction, or any other organized group is more likely to be cohesive.

Virtually all the legislative properties and attributes already discussed affect cohesion. A small-sized legislature, for example, is likely to be more cohesive than a larger one because there is more face-to-face communication. Similarly, the more structurally integrated the parts of a legislature are, the greater is the probability of achieving the coordinated actions that, in turn, contribute to cohesiveness. Shared group-relevant values, attitudes, and goals, which increase cooperative behavior, also are likely to increase the cohesion of a legislative body. Finally, shared acceptance of legislative norms and rules about interpersonal and collective behavior, tend to increase normativeness, and would appear to be associated with cohesiveness.

## FACTORS INFLUENCING THE BEHAVIOR OF INDIVIDUAL LEGISLATORS

Having discussed certain properties and attributes of legislatures which are assumed to affect behavior en masse we now turn to the behavior of the individual legislator.

In a comprehensive review of research in legislative behavior, John C. Wahlke[12] distinguished three general types of studies that have been carried out:

1. Studies that ascertain certain demographic characteristics of the membership of particular representative bodies.[13]

2. Studies that seek to explain the action of representatives in the form of general propositions about their behavior as individuals. This category includes:

a. Studies that try to measure the proportionate influence of different forces suspected of affecting legislative behavior, that is, mass media, letters from constituents, and so forth.[14]

b. Studies that attempt to examine representatives' behavior in terms of the theories and concepts of general psychology.[15]

c. Studies that describe the relationship of representatives to their political parties,[16] to pressure groups,[17] to other legislators,[18] to their constituencies,[19] and to cultural environment.[20]

d. Studies that seek to compare the influence of party, constituency, and so forth on the individual legislator.[21]

e. Studies that examine the effect of the formation of personal friendships or the development of subject matter *expertise* on legislative behavior.[22]

3. Studies that focus upon the actions in which members of a given body engage simultaneously and collectively.[23]

Wahlke[24] argues that although many of these studies are both sophisticated in conception and rigorous in design, they employ such a diversity of terms and concepts and focus on such a variety of questions that it is very difficult to cumulate them into any concise and coherent statements of the present status of knowledge. He sees as a reason for this the frequent failure of these studies to use a carefully formulated and clearly recognized model of the representative actor. This results in the implicit use of a great variety of models. He offers, as a solution to this problem, the adoption of the role concept for the study of legislators' behavior:

> Role has been used with relatively minor variations of meaning by analysts in sociology, anthropology, and social psychology which indicates its probable utility for tying together the concern of institutional, functional and behavioral studies in political science. Better than any alternative concept in social science, the notion of role yields a model of the legislator as an acting human individual which is consistent with the basic understandings of individual and group psychology and at the same time yields a model of the legislature as an institutionalized human group which logically incorporates the model of the individual legislator and which relates the behavior of legislators to the problems of legislative structure and function which are the traditional concern of students in the field.

In their study of four American state legislatures, Wahlke, Eulau, Ferguson, and Buchanan[25] suggested that it was analytically possible to distinguish three legislative role sectors: the core roles, consisting of the purposive, representational and consensual roles; the clientele role, which focused on the legislator's relations with party, pressure groups, and administration; and the incidental roles which focused on the effect of kinship, friendship, and group membership in the legislative system.

In this study we describe "purposive roles" as "goals." With respect to other role sectors, we focus only on representational roles per se. Yet we agree with Wahlke and his associates and with Jewell and Patterson[26] that legislative behavior best can be conceptualized as a role or series of roles. Since legislative behavior, in a broad sense, can be viewed as role behavior, it seems appropriate to expand our conception of role and a related concept, reference group.

## ROLE AND REFERENCE GROUP

We define "role" as a set of expectations held for a position by its incumbent and by the incumbents of related positions.[27] A "reference group" is one that serves as either a positive or negative frame of normative reference for a segment of the individual's values.[28] The two concepts, as will be shown, are intimately related.

The position of legislator is both a formal and a highly visible one. Consequently, there are certain forms of behavior that are expected of incumbents, and which may be said to constitute the role associated with the position. The limits within which all occupants are expected to act in order to carry out their particular functions may be termed the "prescribed" part of the role. These prescriptions may be contained in a code of formal rules, they may be a part of the informal "rules of the game," or they may be a combination of both. Formal and informal norms also establish rules of behavior that are prohibited. However, so long as the functions for which the legislative position was set up are reasonably well performed, the incumbent is permitted considerable latitude. Figure 1 is

FIGURE 1. Behavior associated with the legislative role.

| *Prescribed Role Behavior*[a] | | | *Permitted Role Behavior*[b] | | | *Forbidden Role Behavior*[c] | | |
|---|---|---|---|---|---|---|---|---|
| 100 | 75 | 50 | 25 | 0 | $\overline{25}$ | $\overline{50}$ | $\overline{75}$ | $\overline{100}$ |
| Fulfilled Expectations | | | | | | | | Unfulfilled Expectations |

[a] Authoritative decision making and settling of intergroup conflicts.
[b] Performing services for constituents and providing and securing information from interest groups.
[c] Violating formal and informal norms of ethical conduct and conflict of interest.

a schematic representation of possible prescribed, permitted, and prohibited behaviors associated with the legislative role.[29]

It is in the permitted area that we normally get individual variation in legislative role-taking. In part, such variations are functions of individual physiological and personality differences. For instance, one legislator may be robust, hyperactive, cheerful, and optimistic while a party colleague may be just the opposite. Although such physiological and personality differences obviously affect behavior, they are not considered in the present analysis.[30] Rather, the focus here is upon certain cultural and institutional factors affecting variations in role orientations.

## CULTURAL DETERMINANTS

The taking of roles depends on learning to perceive one's self in relation to others. This in turn presupposes the acquisition of group-shared norms and frames of reference, as self-perceptions in relation to others do not occur in a vacuum. The family provides the individual's first frame of reference, and it is as a family member that he acquires many of the values and attitudes that are the foundation of subsequent (including political) behavior.[31] As the individual's contacts spread outside the family he acquires new frames of reference which help determine his attitudes to objects, individuals, and groups in his environment.[32] If he finds his new frames of reference useful, he internalizes them so that they become an essential part of his "performing-perceiving-thinking-feeling process."[33]

Examples, by no means exhaustive, of this category of reference group are school, work, religious, ethnic, interest, social, and extended family groups as well as business and professional associations and political parties. Three brief comments touching upon the definition of reference groups must be made.

First, reference groups, in order to function, need not be membership groups. Thus, an adolescent's political views and perspectives can be influenced by a political party's position even if he is not a formal member of the party. However, the individual is not simply the passive and uncritical recipient of stimuli emitted by reference groups; he may feel that he knows what a group's norms are, but he may reject them. In this event the group actually provides a negative frame of reference.

Second, a reference group's norms generally are not totally relevant for structuring all of one's values and attitudes. A political party's position on the desirability of governmental assistance to the arts may influence the position of a party member on that issue but need not affect his attitude toward what constitutes art. Conversely, certain norms of the Catholic Church can affect one's private view concerning procreation but need not necessarily influence his attitude toward birth control as public policy.

Third, even group norms which have been internalized are not immutable. A person at an early age may have internalized the notion that Negroes are generically different from whites, yet he need not continue to adhere to the norm if, later in life, he is placed in a group environment in which the norm is both rejected and ridiculed.

It seems then, that reference groups affect role behavior both before and after an individual becomes an incumbent of a legislative position. First, they strongly influence role potential (that is, the expectations for the role which an individual brings to the position) because they aid in structuring individual values and perspectives. For example, a legislator who is himself a member of a minority ethnic group may have internalized from that group the notion that a good legislator is one who, first and foremost, articulates the interest of the group. Another individual's model may be predicated on a business group norm, such as the one generally ascribed to a former U.S. Secretary of Defense. Further, a person socialized and elected from a small rural constituency may bring to the legislative position, attitudes toward interest groups that are quite different from those of an individual elected from a large metropolitan area constituency.

However, once he becomes an incumbent, his performance as legislator will be observed and evaluated by groups (such as party colleagues) within the legislative system. As the definition suggests, he attends and is sensitive to the norms and expectations of these new reference groups. Since previous internalized norms are not unchanging, he may restructure some of his initial expectations for the position. For example, he may have to revise an expectation that he will be directly involved in policymaking, if he finds that his party expects policy innovation to be left to the party leaders. Or he may find that large numbers, limited available time, and a seniority norm preclude anything but minimal discussion of public policy. An expectation of specializing in a substantive legislative area such as foreign relations also may be revised if the individual finds there is no possibility of obtaining a seat on the legislative committee concerned with foreign relations. Similarly, a perceived role as "tribune of the people" may have to be restructured in terms of a prevailing prescription that freshmen legislators must be seen frequently but heard seldom.

This is not to suggest that the new legislator's attitudes toward the expectations held for him will always be one of uncritical acceptance. At times, their norms may be only segmentally relevant, as would be the case if a legislator were willing to act cohesively with his party colleagues only on organization matters. He may even reject a new norm or expectation entirely. Thus, he may refuse to serve a period of apprenticeship, to "get along by going along," if he believes that such behavior will result in his subsequent electoral defeat.

Legislative role orientation, and hence behavior, is thus a product of both initial expectations held by an individual for the legislative position, and attitudes and perspectives subsequently developed in response to the expectations and requirements of significant "others" interacting with him in the legislative system. In effect, this is a combination of what Eulau and Hinckley[34] termed the two principle models of legislative behavior. The first, the "outside" model, conceives of legislative behavior as a product of forces or influences outside the institutional boundaries of the legislature (for example, constituency and pressure groups). The second, the "inside" model, sees behavior revealed in the formal and informal substructures, and authority relations and influence patterns within the legislature itself.

Underlying the outside model, although it is rarely if ever stated explicitly is the assumption that within any society the distinctive subcultural value patterns which have been internalized by legislators before they take office are sufficiently pervasive, as to result in genuine differences in behavior, regardless of the institutional arrangement of the legislative system. Thus, behavior within the legislature largely is determined not by the existing structure or its norms, but by cultural differences among the individual legislators. The assumption underlying the inside model is that in any society the norms prescribing the behavior associated with the legislative position are so visible and so widely shared, that behavior within the legislature is virtually impervious to subcultural influences stemming from differences in the backgrounds of the legislative actors. In other words, it matters little what the backgrounds and expectations of legislators are, as their behavior is determined largely by existing constitutional arrangements and by the legislative structure. In opting for a theory which combines both outside and inside models, we really are rejecting their underlying assumptions taken individually. Thus, we begin the analysis of this particular legislative body by delineating the legislators' ethnic, religious, occupational, and educational backgrounds as well as describing such prelegislative experiences as times and agents of their initial political interest (political socialization), patterns of political recruitment, preparliamentary political experience, and the circumstances and motives that inspired their candidacies. In keeping with our theory that expectations for the legislative position generated by prelegislative experiences such as those just described, in part determine subsequent legislative behavior, we look at how examples of behavioral differences, specifically, legislators' goals and representational role orientations, are associated with variations in the respondents' backgrounds and prelegislative experiences. But, as it was theorized that attitudes and perspectives developed after incumbency in response to the expectations of significant other groups (such as party and constituency) also help determine legislators' behaviors, variations in their goals and representational role orientations also are cross-tabulated with left–right party differences and the political competitiveness and relative urbanism of their constituencies. A type of partial correlation analysis is employed to suggest which prelegislative and postlegislative experience variables are the best predictors of legislators' goals and representational roles. It should be noted that we will employ party affiliation and constituency differences as postincumbency variables because it is assumed that they become particularly salient at that time, in that legislators may very well restructure some initial expectations for their roles as a consequence of interactions qua legislators with party colleagues and constituents.[35]

In this section we have discussed legislative attributes and behavior in very general terms. In the next chapter we narrow our concern and focus upon such attributes and behavior as they are manifested in the Canadian parliamentary system. The remaining chapters generally are given over to the analysis of a particular Canadian House of Commons.

## Notes

1. Benjamin Jowett (trans.), *The Basic Works of Aristotle,* (ed.), Richard McKean (New York: Random House, Inc., 1941), p. 1200.

2. In 1958, Warren E. Miller and Donald E. Stokes interviewed a sample of the 85th Congress. The only reports of this research published when this book was being written were "Constituency Influence in Congress," *American Political Science Review,* **55** (1961), 345–357, and the important "Party Government and the Saliency of Congress," *Public Opinion Quarterly,* **26** (1962), 531–546. Charles L. Clapp's valuable work, *The Congressman: His Work as He Sees It* (Washington: Brookings Institute, 1963) is based largely on interviews and group discussions in 1959 with thirty-six members of the House of Representatives. Unfortunately, no quantitative data are presented that could be compared with our findings. Such data, based upon interviews with 118 Congressmen in 1963–1964, are presented by Roger H. Davidson, David M. Kovenock, and Michael O'Leary in *Congress in Crisis: Politics and Congressional Reform* (Belmont, Calif.: Wadsworth, 1966). See also Roger H. Davidson, "Congress and the Executive: The Race for Representation," in Alfred deGrazia (ed.), *Congress: The First Branch of Government* (Washington: American Enterprise Institute for Public Policy Research, 1966), pp. 377–414. Outside of North America, a study involving interviews with a sample of seventy-five members of the French National Assembly drawn from the Union for the New Republic, the Socialist, and the Popular Republican Movement parties was carried out in 1960 by William H. Hunt. Duncan MacRae has employed quantitative methods to study French Chambers of Deputies during the 4th Republic, but no published reports of either author's work were available when the present study was in preparation.

3. John Wahlke points out a number of cogent reasons for studying legislative bodies in John Wahlke, *The Legislative System: Explorations in Legislative Behavior* (New York: John Wiley and Sons, Inc., 1962), pp. 5–7.

4. Malcolm E. Jewell and Samuel C. Patterson ascribe the following functions to legislatures: conflict management, under which is subsumed, deliberative, decisional, adjudicative, and cathartic functions; and integration of the polity which subsumes authorization, legitimation, and representation. See Malcolm E. Jewell and Samuel C. Patterson, *The Legislative Process in the United States* (New York: Random House, Inc., 1966), pp. 5–25.

5. Talcott Parsons, "Voting and the Equilibrium of the American Political System," *American Voting Behavior* (eds.), Eugene Burdick and Arthur J. Brodbeck (New York: The Free Press, 1959), pp. 80–141.

6. For a discussion of this see Duncan MacRae, *The Dimensions of Congressional Voting: A Statistical Study of the House of Representatives in the Eighty-first Congress* (Berkeley, Calif.: University of California Press, 1958) or David Truman, *The Congressional Party* (New York: John Wiley and Sons, Inc., 1959).

7. Norbert Weiner, quoted in Karl W. Deutch, *The Nerves of Government* (New York: The Free Press, 1963), p. 77.

8. See Bertram M. Gross, *The Legislative Struggle* (New York: McGraw-Hill, Inc., 1953).

9. Theodore Newcomb, Ralph Turner, and Philip Converse, *Social Psychology: The Study of Human Interaction* (New York: Holt, Rinehart and Winston, Inc., 1965), p. 376.

10. In his study of the United States Senate, Donald R. Matthews listed six categories of informal norms recognized by Senators: apprenticeship, legislative work, specialization, courtesy, reciprocity, and institutional patriotism. See Donald R. Matthews, "The Folkways of the United States Senate: Conformity to Group Norms and Legislative Effectiveness," *American Political Science Review,* **53** (1959), 1064–1089. John Wahlke and LeRoy Ferguson categorized informal norms in terms of the following functions: rules that promote group cohesion, rules that promote predictability in behavior, rules that expedite legislative business, rules that serve to give tactical advantages, and desirable personal qualities cited as rules. See John Wahlke and LeRoy Ferguson, "Rules of the Game," in John Wahlke *et al., The Legislative System* (New York: John Wiley and Sons, Inc., 1962), pp. 141–169.

11. For the body of legislators whose behavior is the subject of this book, the author found that informal norms apparently decreased conflict, expedited the flow of legislation, discouraged personal conduct that would subject the legislature to external criticism, helped propagate the party system and party solidarity, and encouraged *expertise* and adherence to formal rules. See Allan Kornberg, "The Rules of the Game in the Canadian House of Commons," *Journal of Politics,* **26** (1964), 358–380.

12. John Wahlke, "Behavioral Analyses of Representative Bodies," a paper delivered at the International Political Science Association Conference in Ann Arbor, Michigan in September 1960. Now published in Austin Ranney (ed.), *Essays in the Behavioral Study of Politics* (Urbana, Ill.: University of Illinois Press, 1962), pp. 173–190.

13. Mattei Dogan, "Political Assent in a Class Society: French Deputies, 1870–1958," *Political Decision Makers* (ed.), Dwaine Marvick (New York: The Free Press, 1961), pp. 57–90. Only one example for each type of study is given here because we have two excellent surveys of the literature. The first is the aforementioned article by Wahlke. The other survey was performed by Norman C. Meller, "Legislative Behavior Research," *Western Political Quarterly,* **14** (1960), 131–153, and "Legislative Behavior Research Revisited: A Review of Five Years' Publications," *Western Political Quarterly,* **18** (1965), 776–793. There is also the outstanding bibliographical essay by Heinz Eulau and Katherine Hinckley, "Legislative Institutions and Processes" in James A. Robinson (ed.), *Political Science Annual 1966* (New York: Bobbs-Merrill Company, Inc., 1966), pp. 85–190. See also, "The Legislative Process: A Bibliography in Legislative Behavior," Bibliographic Series No. 8, (Michigan State University: Institute for Community Development and Services, 1963).

14. Lewis A. Dexter, "What Do Congressmen Hear?" in Nelson Posby *et al.* (eds.), *Politics and Social Life* (Boston, Mass.: Houghton Mifflin Company, 1963), pp. 485–495.

15. James D. Barber, *The Lawmakers: Recruitment and Adaptation to Legislative Life* (New Haven, Conn.: Yale University Press, 1965).

16. Frank J. Sorauf, *Party and Representation: Legislative Politics in Pennsylvania* (New York: Atherton Press, 1963).

17. Samuel C. Patterson, "The Role of the Lobbyist: The Case of Oklahoma," *Journal of Politics,* **25** (February 1963), 72–92.

18. Donald R. Matthews, *United States Senators and Their World* (New York: Vintage Books, 1960), pp. 102–117.

19. Wilder W. Crane, Jr., "Do Representatives Represent?" *Journal of Politics,* **22** (1960), 295–299.

20. Edward A. Shils, "The Legislator and His Environment," *University of Chicago Law Review,* **18** (1951), 571–584.

21. Thomas A. Flinn, "Party Responsibility in the States: Some Causal Factors," *American Political Science Review,* **58** (1964), 60–71.

22. William Buchanan, "The Bonds of Friendship," and "Subject Matter Experts," both in John Wahlke *et al., The Legislative System: Explorations in Legislative Behavior* (New York: John Wiley and Sons, Inc., 1962), pp. 193–235.

23. James A. Robinson, *The Role of the Rules Committee* (Indianapolis, Ind.: Bobbs-Merrill Company, Inc., 1963).

24. John Wahlke, "Behavioral Analysis of Representative Bodies," p. 7.

25. Wahlke, pp. 3–29.

26. Jewell and Patterson, p. 17.

27. Even a cursory review of the literature on role reveals that the use made of the concept in great part depends upon one's theoretical preference and the nature of one's discipline. The pioneer works in role were carried out by George Herbert Mead in *Mind, Self and Society* (Chicago, Ill.: University of Chicago Press, 1934) and Ralph Linton, *The Study of Man* (New York: Appleton-Century-Crofts, 1936), pp. 133–140. Role has been utilized so differently in research that Lionel J. Newman and James W. Hughes in their survey of the literature for the years 1900–1950 in "The Problem of the Concept of Role: A Re-Survey of the Literature," *Social Forces,* **30** (1951–1952), 141–149, suggest three classifications for the various definitions employed by anthropologists, sociologists, and psychologists. Neal Gross, Ward S. Mason, and Alexander McEachern also suggest three categories into which definitions of role may be classified in *Explorations in Role Analysis* (New York: John Wiley and Sons, Inc., 1956), pp. 11–18. Other surveys of the literature on role include Theodore Sarbin, "Role Theory," in Gardner Lindzey (ed.), *Handbook of Social Psychology, I* (Reading, Mass.: Addison-Wesley Publishing Company, 1954), pp. 223–258, and Fredrich Bate, "Position Role and Status: A Reformulation of Concepts," *Social Forces,* **34** (1956), 159–163. See also the works of Talcott Parsons and Edward A. Shils, *Toward a General Theory of Action* (Cambridge, Mass.: Harvard University Press, 1951); Theodore Newcomb, *Social Psychology* (New York: Holt, Rinehart and Winston, Inc., 1950), and Theodore Newcomb, Ralph H. Turner, and Phillip E. Converse, *Social Psychology: The Study of Human Interaction* (New York: Holt, Rinehart and Winston, Inc., 1965).

28. Both the role and reference group definitions employed here are based on the more elaborate definitions of Simon D. Perry, "Conflict of Expectations and Role in Policy Science Behavior" (Doctoral dissertation, Michigan State University, 1961), pp. 13–39.

Herbert Hyman was among the first to use the concept reference group. It has been effectively developed in the works of Muzafer Sherif, "The Concept of Reference Group in Human Relations," in *Group Relations at the Crossroads,* Muzafer Sherif and M. O. Wilson (eds.) (New York: Harper & Row, Publishers, 1953), pp. 203–231; Robert K. Merton and Alice Kitt, "Contribution to the Theory of Reference Group Behavior," in Robert K. Merton and Paul Lazarsfeld (eds.), *Continuity in Social Research* (New York: The Free Press, 1950); Harold

H. Kelley, "Two Functions of Reference Groups," in Guy Swanson, Theodore Newcomb, and Eugene Hartley (eds.), *Readings in Social Psychology* (New York: Holt, Rinehart and Winston, Inc., 1952), pp. 410–414; Tamotsu Shibutani, "Reference Groups as Perspectives," *American Journal of Sociology,* **60** (1955), 562–569; and Ralph H. Turner, "Role-Taking, Role Standpoint, and Reference-Group Behavior," *American Journal of Sociology,* **61** (1956), 316–328.

29. The diagram is based on Figure 11.1 in Newcomb, Turner, and Converse, *Social Psychology* (Holt, Rinehart and Winston, Inc., 1965), p. 328.

30. For an impressive study of legislative behavior in which these differences are dealt with see David J. Barber, *The Lawmakers: Recruitment and Adaptation to Legislative Life* (New Haven, Conn.: Yale University Press, 1965).

31. See, for example, Herbert McClosky and Harold Dahlgren, "Primary Group Influence on Party Loyalty," *American Political Science Review,* **53** (1959), 757–776, and Robert E. Lane, "Fathers and Sons: Foundations of Political Belief," *American Sociological Review,* **24** (1959), 502–511.

32. Georg Karlsson, "Political Attitudes among Male Swedish Youth," *Acta Sociologica,* **3** (1958), 1–24.

33. Theodore Newcomb, *Social Psychology* (New York: Holt, Rinehart and Winston, Inc., 1950), p. 224.

34. Eulau and Hinckley, "Legislative Institutions and Processes," p. 87.

35. Party and constituency also are important reference groups for structuring the values, attitudes, and expectations of legislators for the position of MP, long before they take their seats in parliament.

# 2

# The Canadian Parliamentary System

The foundations for the cultural and economic regionalism that still affects Canada were laid long before the Dominion of Canada formally came into being with the passage of the British North America (BNA) Act by an Imperial Parliament on July 1, 1867. Because this is a study of legislative behavior in a Canadian House of Commons, we can describe neither the events and conditions leading to the birth of the Canadian nation, nor selected aspects of Canadian history subsequent to that climacteric.[1] Rather, the focus will be on the formal powers allocated by the BNA Act (the written portion of the Canadian Constitution) to the national government; the institutions and procedures which have evolved in order to realize these powers; the political parties which breathe life into the legislative system; and the impact of the cultural cleavage between Quebec and English-speaking Canada upon the parliamentary process.

## THE POWER OF THE NATIONAL GOVERNMENT

In contrast to and, presumably, as a result of American experience with federalism, the framers of the BNA Act created what they assumed was a strong central government. To the provincial governments they allocated only sixteen powers, which, in the words of Section 92: 16 were of a "merely local or private nature in the province." On the other hand, they allocated very substantial powers (express, general, and residual) to the national government. These are set out in Section 91, and begin with the preamble that parliament shall make laws for "the Peace, Order, and good Government of Canada, in relation to all Matters, not coming within the Classes of Subjects by the Act assigned exclusively to the Legislatures of the Provinces." In addition to these already formidable powers, parliament also was to exercise concurrent jurisdiction with the provinces over agriculture and immigration with the federal powers prevailing in the event of conflict (Section 95). However, the provinces did not become mere ciphers, in part because of the restraint exercised by successive national governments,[2] and in part because judicial interpretation of the provincial power to regulate property and civil rights greatly expanded the scope of provincial authority. Thus the Canadian provinces exercise as much or more power vis à vis their national government than do the states in the American federal system.

The parliament, which would carry out the powers allocated to the national government under the BNA Act, was to consist of an executive and a bicameral legislature. Not unnaturally, in light of Canada's colonial status at the time, the executive was to be the British Monarch whose prerogative powers were to be exercised by the Crown's representative, the Governor-General. These prerogatives are outlined in the *Letters Patent* last revised in 1947. Although even today, in theory, all acts of Parliament are proclaimed and all appointments are made on behalf of the Queen and Governor-General, in actual practice the executive powers of government have, since 1926, rested in the hands of the Prime Minister and his Cabinet.[3]

## STRUCTURE

### THE CABINET

The Cabinet formulates and carries out all executive policies, exercises virtual control over all financial matters, assembles the legislative proposals that Parliament considers, and serves as the political head of the several departments of government. As is the custom in British parliamentary systems, the current Prime Minister is the head of the political party that was victorious in the last national election. Except in the case of formal coalitions, the Prime Minister selects his Cabinet colleagues from among the members of his parliamentary party. He determines how many will serve, coordinates their professional interactions, moves them from portfolio to portfolio and, occasionally, requests their resignations. Although nominally the servant of the House of Commons, as it remains in office only as long as it retains the support of a majority of House members, the Cabinet in a very real sense is both leader and master of that body. There is some dispute over who is or who is not actually in a Canadian Cabinet.[4] At the time these interviews were taken there were twenty-two heads of various departments and sixteen parliamentary secretaries assisting the ministers. (These will be termed the "Administration," and may be seen as performing both essentially integrative and disruptive functions.) The Administration integrates in that its legislative proposals constitute the bulk of the subject matter which will concern everyone—members of both the governing and the opposition parties—during the life of a Parliament. Not only does it decide what everyone will do, it also determines the order in which everything will be done and, in great part, the amount of time which will be spent on every item of business. These same proposals, however, also generate most of the conflict between the governing and opposition parties, and thus disrupt the functioning of Parliament as an organization.

A position in the Administration provides an opportunity to specialize and to acquire *expertise* in substantive areas such as finance and defense to a limited number of members of the governing party. Although, theoretically Administration members are "generalists" who can be expected to perform with equal facility in any one of several departments and who, therefore, leave technical matters to the professionals in their departmental bureaucracies, in actual practice their executive roles require them either to have,[5] or to acquire rapidly, a considerable body of specialized knowledge. This is also the case with their counterparts and critics in the opposition parties. The latter's positions as front-benchers and, ultimately, their aspirations for executive office, in part depend upon the quality of their criticism and hence upon specialized knowledge.

The above discussion has suggested yet another function performed by the Administration—that of providing a motive to act in concert with one's party. Because the pinnacle of a parliamentary career presumably is an appointment to the Cabinet, and because such appointments normally are given only to loyal and dependable party members, the individual MP is provided with a powerful incentive to remain faithful to his party. According to Dawson and Ward,[6] older MP's, although they rarely receive

Cabinet appointments, are induced to remain loyal because they still can "look forward to a possible position on a prominent board or commission, a judgeship, or most coveted of all by those in whom ambition has languished, a senatorship." It is to a brief consideration of the Senate, the Upper House of the Canadian Parliament, that we must now turn.

## THE SENATE

After a century, the Canadian Senate is unique among parliamentary second chambers in that it has retained a full set of legislative muscles, but consistently has refused to make real use of them.

Like its American counterpart, the Senate had its origin in the colonial legislative councils. The fathers of Confederation perceived it as the "house which has the sober second thought in legislation."[7] Supposedly, it also guaranteed provincial and regional rights while a large property qualification for appointed members insured, in the words of Canada's first Prime Minister, John A. Macdonald,[8] that "the Upper House . . . is then the representative of property." Finally, the luxury of life tenure presumably would encourage Senators to perform their quasi-judicial roles in a wholly impartial manner. Despite these responsibilities, and the veto power over Commons legislation which it was given, there is little doubt that the Senate initially was envisaged as a second chamber and not as the competitor of the popularly elected House of Commons. This is evident in the constitutional requirement that all "money bills"—the bulk of any legislative program—originate in the Commons.

In the years immediately following Confederation, the Senate was the epitomy of nineteenth century liberalism, as many of the incumbents were pioneers who had fought their way to success and prominence through their own efforts. Later, however, inferior partisan appointments, the centralization of leadership in a not conspicuously able oligarchy, and the concomitant failure to make use of the available human resources lead to a serious decline in the quality of the Senate. Consistent demands were made, particularly by progressive critics, for either a drastic reform or the abolition of the Red Chamber.

Historically, the Senate has been extremely reluctant to interfere with the popular will insofar as that will is expressed by the House of Commons. According to Mackay,[9] from 1867 to 1960 the Senate amended approximately 20 percent and rejected only 3 percent of the bills coming to it from the Commons. Although it has been commended for relieving the Commons of considerable work by hearing in committee the testimony of interest groups' representatives on important pieces of legislation; for improving the grammar and wording of bills originating in the Commons; and, increasingly, for concerning itself with the problem of the domination by the Cabinet of the House of Commons,[10] two serious handicaps limit its effectiveness. First, the Senate has only a limited amount of serious work at the beginning of a parliamentary session when legislation has not yet passed the Commons. Then it is inundated by bills from the House toward the end of a session. Consequently, the "sober second look" it was intended to take at important legislation, at best, tends to be more of a fleeting glance. Second, most of the work which *is* undertaken by the Senate is carried out (as measured by attendance and participation in debate) by a small group of fifteen or twenty individuals.[11] As the participation of the majority of the Senate in the Canadian legislative process is sufficiently limited, the focus will be exclusively on the House of Commons.

## HOUSE OF COMMONS

### *Recruitment of Personnel*

Theoretically, the parliamentary recruitment channel is open in that anyone twenty-one years of age or older who can persuade twenty-five voters in a district to sign his nomination papers, and who is able to raise the necessary deposit ($200) can become a candidate for the House of Commons. In practice, the channel is considerably narrower as it tends to be controlled by the several constituency organizations of the four national parties. The individuals whom the local parties recruit for the position, although in certain respects representative of a cross section of the population, nevertheless are drawn from the upper social strata of Canadian society. Regionally, all but the Social Credit party tend to recruit their most prestigious candidates from Quebec, and their least prestigious from the Maritime and Western provinces.

It would appear that, in comparison with other national legislatures in Western countries, recruits for the House of Commons tend to be relatively young men who enjoy only limited periods of tenure in Parliament. Dawson and Ward[12] claim that rarely is the turnover in the House membership after a national election less than 40 percent, and that only 8–10 percent of any current crop of legislators have had ten or more years of parliamentary experience. Sociologist John Porter[13] has argued that the weakness exhibited by the Canadian parties in the late 1950s was a function of the lack of seasoned political leadership, particularly, in the Liberal party. He said very few were "political men" in that they had made a career out of politics. Liberal leaders were coopted for a brief stint from either the business world or the bureaucracy and then returned to their previous domains. Although one might dispute Porter's tendency to generalize to all parties on the basis of the Liberal party, still in comparison to their counterparts in the American Congress the careers of Canadian MPs probably are brief. In a comparative study of a group of leaders from the 88th Congress and from Canada's 25th Parliament, Norman C. Thomas and the author were impressed by the sharp difference in the experience of the two groups. In Canada, fully 80 percent of the leaders had less than thirteen years of experience in Parliament, whereas, 95 percent of the Americans had served for that length of time. Consequently, there was a highly significant correlation of Gamma = 0.92[14] between legislative experience and national background of leaders. In comparison with nonleaders, however, the Canadian parliamentary leaders had enjoyed a fairly long period of tenure. For example, 64 percent of the leaders had served at least seven years in Parliament, but only 12 percent of the nonleaders had enjoyed equally long careers. As legislative longevity is, in part, a function of interparty competitiveness, it was not surprising that there was also a strong correlation (Gamma =0.52) between this variable and parliamentary experience. The implication of these and other aspects of recruitment for the operation of the Canadian House of Commons will be discussed in a later section.

*Size*

The Commons today is a body of 265 members elected by plurality voting from 263 electoral districts.[15] The districts are apportioned by province, and range in size from the tiny (12,000 people) and completely rural Ile-de-la-Madelaine to suburban York-Scarborough with a population of 267,000. This variation in the population of electoral districts traditionally has been justified on the grounds that: (1) rural areas ought to be overrepresented, and (2) some malapportionment was preferable to the dismemberment of established municipalities and counties. It was not until the 1960s that really serious consideration was given to a reapportionment of federal constituencies which would reflect the distribution of the national population.[16] When this reapportionment is accomplished, representation in the House of Commons will reflect even more the dominance of the Canadian Federal Union by the central provinces of Quebec and Ontario. At the time this study was undertaken, these two provinces contained 63 percent of the national population, and they elected 60 percent of the MPs (see Table 2.1).

With 265 members, the House of Commons is large enough to have available at any one time a substantial pool of highly educated individuals who possess a variety of specialized skills. (The level of the skills that they can bring to bear on problems can be inferred from the data to be presented in the next chapter.) Although large enough in terms of available human resources, the House still affords excellent opportunities for a variety of interpersonal communications. The offices of individuals in the same party normally are grouped in particular areas, but all MPs, regardless of party, continually meet in such places as the tunnel connecting the West and Center Blocks, the elevators, the parliamentary restaurants, and at the numerous social events to which they are invited because of their official status. In fact, in our view, there may be too much interaction outside the House because tensions built up during a sitting (which ordinarily might dissipate if legislators were not brought into almost continuous contact) frequently tend to remain and to cumulate.

TABLE 2.1 Distribution of National Population, Seats in the House of Commons, and Study Sample by Region[a] (percentage)

| *Region* | *National Population* | *Seats in the House of Commons* | *Study Sample* |
|---|---|---|---|
| Maritime Provinces | 10 | 13 | 12 |
| Central Provinces | 63 | 60 | 62 |
| Western Provinces | 27 | 27 | 26 |
| | (*N* = 18, 238, 247) | (*N* = 265) | (*N* = 165) |

[a] Data on distribution of population and seats in the Commons are derived from *Population of Electoral Districts* (Ottawa: Dominion Bureau of Statistics, 1961). Maritime Provinces include Newfoundland, Prince Edward Island, Nova Scotia, and New Brunswick. Western Provinces include the Yukon and Northwest Territories as well as Manitoba, Saskatchewan, Alberta, and British Columbia.

The House of Commons, then, is of ideal size in that it is large enough to bring to bear sufficient specialized skills and aptitudes required for solving difficult problems, but small enough to permit considerable person-to-person interaction and, potentially, the formation of a large network of close interpersonal relationships. Despite this theoretical advantage, the British model parliamentary system in no small way precludes the formation of such a network on a cross-party basis.

### *Procedure*

FORMAL AND INFORMAL NORMS Procedure consists of the patterns of activities prescribed by a set of formal and informal norms which the members of a legislative body follow in carrying out their tasks. Procedural norms are functional for maintaining the viability of the legislature as an organization because they both enable it to achieve its goals and to regularize and make predictable the interpersonal relations of legislators. The bulk of Canadian parliamentary procedure, like the institution itself, was transplanted from Great Britain. Over the years, however, certain routines have been developed that are indigenous to the Canadian system. The formal sources for parliamentary procedure, in addition to the BNA Act, are the Standing Orders of both the Commons and Senate, certain acts of past Parliaments, the written work of recognized authorities on the parliamentary system, and the rulings of past Speakers. In situations not covered by these sources, the House falls back on any relevant Canadian or, if need be, British parliamentary traditions. Thus, by tradition, an MP is never referred to by name in a debate, but rather by his constituency (the Honorable member from ———) or by formal position (the Honorable, the Minister) of Agriculture). By tradition, also, members do not publicly question the integrity of other members, nor do they accuse them of deliberately making false statements in the House.

Since a British model parliamentary system, in order to achieve its goals, must evaluate the legislative proposals of the Government, the formal rules of procedure facilitate the passage of a Government program. In no small part, this is accomplished by limiting debate on the proposals, particularly among back bench legislators. Thus, the formal rules of debate require that legislators speak only once to a question; that their remarks be relevant to the subject being discussed; that speeches cannot be read; and, if the legislator is not a Cabinet Minister or the Leader of the Opposition,[17] that he limit his remarks to thirty minutes. Two procedural devices ("closure" and "putting the previous question") also are available to the Government to insure that debate on an issue ultimately will end.[18] In addition, certain informal arrangements such as the pairing of individuals on opposite sides of a question, and the agreements that are reached among the several party Whips and the Speaker's Chair on the frequency and order of speakers, also limit broad participation in debate as they at once encourage absenteeism, and discourage requests to be heard publicly.

Both an informal and formal sanction system are available to enforce the norms. An offending member may be socially ostracized or he may find it difficult to speak in the House because the Speaker will refuse to recognize him.[19] A more formal sanction is to be "named" or to temporarily be expelled from the House by him. Really serious breaches of the norms, such as lying in the House, or making false charges against another member, are referred to a "privileges" committee and since the House, like most democratic legislatures, is a judge of its members, in the extreme case, the offender may be permanently expelled.

There is some question, in view of the large turnover in membership, the vituperative character of debate, and the presumably obstructive behavior of opposition parties, as to how effective are both the norms and sanctions systems within the Commons. The large proportion of new members and the general low level of parliamentary experience which seem to be characteristic of the Canadian House of Commons suggest that neither norms nor sanctions are highly visible to all. Many members may be only vaguely aware or not at all aware of the norms, or the norms may not be enforced with sufficient stringency. This is an area of Canadian legislative behavior that certainly requires additional research.

COOPERATIVE AND COMPETITIVE BEHAVIOR As is the case in all legislatures modeled on the British, House deliberations are presided over by a Speaker. Customarily, French Canadians and English Canadians alternate in this office. Ethnic balance also is maintained by selecting a French Canadian as Deputy-Speaker when the Speaker is English. Unlike the custom in Great Britain, the Speaker is not unopposed in his constituency.[20] Theoretically, he is elected by a majority of the members of the House at the commencement of a new Parliament. In practice, he is the choice of the majority party, although normally a final selection is not made until informal consultations have ensued among the floor leaders of the several parties. Ideally, the Speaker, through his firmness and complete impartiality, has the confidence and respect of legislators that is required for the legislature to function effectively. Unfortunately, not all Speakers are so gifted, and the task of the Canadian Speaker is made more difficult in conflict situations by the fact that all know he owes his position to his party colleagues. Further, unlike British practice, until June, 1965, his rulings were not final but were subject to an appeal to the House as a whole. Frequent appeals from the Speaker's rulings by opposition party members were not conducive to mitigating conflict, and probably were not unrelated to the vituperative debates which increasingly are characteristic of the Canadian House of Commons.[21]

After the election of a Speaker, there ensues the ritual of the Speech from the Throne. The Government's legislative proposals for any session are contained in this speech which is delivered to the combined House and Senate by the Governor-General. At the conclusion of the speech, two newly elected members of the governing party customarily make congratulatory speeches known as the Address in Reply to the Speech from the Throne. The Leader of the Official Opposition then rises and delivers a general critique of the Government's legislative program, and ends by moving a "want of confidence" motion. This is followed by another general criticism of the Government offered by a second opposition party leader, again, culminating in a no-confidence motion. After this motion has been debated and disposed of, another opposition party offers a new subamendment with the same results. The initial motion by the Leader of the Official Opposition is then dealt with.

The various no-confidence motions enable a substantial number of legislators in both governing and opposition parties to speak either in defense of or in opposition to the Government's proposals. Should any of these confidence motions carry, the Government, of course, would resign. In fact (assuming the governing party is in the majority) they do not, and the debate on the Speech from the Throne really serves two purposes. First, the general discussion of public policy permits the Commons to educate a supposedly attentive electorate. Second, in permitting either new members, or back bench members, or both to participate more or less meaningfully in policy evaluation, the speech from the Throne performs a valuable social-psychological function during a parliamentary session.

There are two other opportunities for broad public participation by MPs in policy evaluations. These arise when the House resolves itself into either a Committee of Supply or a Committee of Ways and Means. The Committee of Supply provides an opportunity for the House to evaluate (in theory, to control) the annual expenditures proposed by the Administration. The Administration is required to set forth detailed estimates of the funds that will be required by its several departments during a fiscal year. Technically, each item is debatable when, on the request of the governing party, the House resolves itself into a Committee of Supply. However, the increased scope of governmental activities and the complexity of the subjects with which it is concerned have forced the legislature to streamline these debates Whereas the estimates of only one department could be considered at any one time prior to 1955, the estimate of three now can be considered on each of six motions made by this committee. Debate on each department's estimates usually takes the form of a general criticism and defense of the first item of the estimate by Government and opposition party leaders.

The House, at the request of the Minister of Finance, also resolves itself annually (March or April) into a Committee of Ways and Means. This is the traditional "budget debate" which again provides the governing party with the opportunity to defend, and the opposition parties to criticize what in effect is the Administration's conduct of national affairs. During the course of debate on the budget resolutions (which since 1955 has been limited to eight days) a series of amendments and subamendments expressing want of confidence in the Administration's financial policies are made and invariably voted down.

The constitution (Secs. 53 and 54) requires that all money bills must originate in the Commons with the Government. Thus the opportunity for the ordinary MP, regardless of party, to actually initiate a piece of legislation is limited to eight days during a session (six Tuesdays and two Thursdays) when private members' public bills are considered. Ordinary members also may introduce resolutions that are policy proposals by moving that the Government consider the advisability of these proposals; in effect, that the Government make them a part of its legislative program.

A final opportunity for gratifying individual member participation in legislative affairs and for generating interparty conflict is provided by the daily afternoon "question" period. Technically, such questions to the Administration are asked before the first "Order" for any day, and are referred to as questions asked on the Orders of the Day. That they almost always produce heated, if not enlightened, interchanges[22] between the members of the governing and opposition parties is attested to by the presence in the parliamentary galleries of the largest public audience to the daily proceedings of the Commons. Although they essentially perform a cathartic function for the legislators themselves (to the extent that such exchanges are reported by the mass media) they also may be conceived of as mechanisms for stimulating public interest in the political process.

*Specialization*

THE COMMITTEE SYSTEM The Commons Committees of the Canadian parliamentary system are intended more to facilitate informal debate among members than to serve as forums where the specialized knowledge and *expertise* of legislators can be brought to bear upon particular problems. In committee, members may dispense with the normal requirements that they speak only once and relevantly to a topic, although there is still a time limit (thirty minutes) imposed upon them.

The most frequently employed committee is that of whole house (the Committee of the Whole). Both the aforementioned committees (the Committee of Supply and the Committee of Ways and Means) are committees of the Whole House, and are constituted by a motion from an appropriate minister that the House "resolve itself."

The House also makes limited use of subject matter or standing committees. There were fourteen such committees when the study was carried out, in addition to two committees (the Library Committee and the Printing Committee) with joint Commons-Senate membership. The combined membership is large (thirty-five to sixty) and reflects the distribution of party strength in the House. These committees are chaired by members of the governing party;[23] the members can serve and continue to serve on more than one committee as long as they are re-elected.

Although, theoretically, the standing committees perform both supervisory and investigatory functions (hearing the testimony of expert witnesses and interested parties, subpoenaing records and documents, preparing and writing reports) in practice, their performance has been rather dismal. Dawson and Ward[24] point out that not only do many standing committees meet only infrequently, but in many cases they do not meet at all. When they do meet, they have little of importance to consider, and are hampered in these considerations by a woeful lack of staff assistance. Although Dawson and Ward perceived some changes in this situation occuring during the 24th Parliament (1958–1962), their evaluation of the work of standing committees largely was negative.

The third opportunity for committee work derives from the establishment of *ad hoc* special committees (chiefly investigatory) for the performance of specific and limited tasks. Although at times special committees have been of substantial assistance to the Cabinet in the drafting of new or the modification of existing legislation they do not possess the *expertise* of Royal Commissions and, according to Dawson and Ward,[25] "one of the main tasks of the Committee is the education of its own members." Such a function, however, may be of considerable importance in a legislative system in which 40 percent of the members are novices.

Despite the dearth of any systematic studies,[26] it may be said that the committee system of the Canadian House of Commons affords only a limited opportunity for MPs outside the Administration to develop *expertise* in specialized areas. In comparison to their American counterparts, Canadian standing and special committees[27] cannot be considered efficient mechanisms for performing either investigatory or legislative functions. The several committees of the Whole, although valuable for the cathartic function they perform in permitting a substantial proportion of back benchers to evaluate policy and vent their own and their constituents' grievances against Administration proposals, still do not appear to be the most appropriate vehicles for discharging the basic formal functions of legislation, authorization, and appropriation. The reputed importance of the national bureaucracy in initiating public policy[28] probably is not unrelated to the relative use made of standing committee and committees of the Whole in the Canadian legislative process.

*The Party Caucus.* Normally, each party caucuses once a week. The length of the agenda and the importance of the topics for discussion determine the duration of the meeting. A caucus usually lasts between one and one and one-half hours. When this study was being carried out, the minority Conservative Government was frequently in danger of being overthrown. Consequently, there were sometimes two or even three caucuses during a week in which crucial votes were scheduled. From the interviewees' responses to the question "What do you think are the two or three most important functions a caucus performs?" we can infer that some intraparty opportunities for specializing are available in that 11 percent said a caucus ought to be the place where the reports of special party committees could be read.[29] How extensive these opportunities are, that is, how many such special committees a party employs and the scope and depth of their work unfortunately is not known to us.

### *Cohesion*

In addition to the instances of cooperative behavior among parties already cited, such as the arrangements for the recognition and the order of speakers during debate and the consultation concerning the election of a Speaker, there are other occasions when legislators, regardless of party, act in unison.

Most frequently, these are occasioned by some threat, real or imagined, to their traditional privileges and immunities, or by some questioning or criticism of the honor or integrity of Parliament as an institution. Like most organized groups. MPs are quick to unite against any perceived external threat. In great part, however, most behavior within a British model parliamentary system is competitive. With disciplined parties and infrequent crossing of party lines, it could hardly be otherwise. Thus, it is the parties within the legislature rather than legislature as a whole that act in unison. (In Chapter 7 we explore the respondents' motives for maintaining cohesion.)

*The Party System*

The roots of the two major parties are imbedded in the economic and political struggle which took place in the third decade of the nineteenth century.[30] The Conservative party grew out of the United Empire Loyalist business-professional, established Church elite, which held such a monopoly of the available administrative and judicial offices in the pre-Confederation era that in derision they were termed the Family Compact in Upper Canada (Ontario) and the Chateau Clique in Lower Canada (Quebec). At Confederation, John A. Macdonald[31] was able to unite these groups with the English economic oligarchy and the ultramontane Catholic hierarchy[32] of Quebec into a Conservative party coalition which, except for a five-year period (1873–1878), was to govern the new nation until 1896. The Conservatives, since their National Policy of 1878, have been popularly portrayed with some justification as a high tariff and protectionist party. Their attachment to the British governor of colonial times has endured in their traditional advocacy of close ties with Britain and the Commonwealth. Thus, Conservative party leader Arthur Meighen's reply to a British Prime Minister's request for Canadian troops for use against Turkey in 1922, reportedly was "Ready, aye, ready" whereas William Lyon Mackenzie King, the Liberal leader, answered, "The Canadian Parliament must decide."

The Liberal party's ancestry goes back to a coalition of anti-Catholic, nonestablished church, radical reformers of rural western Ontario, the so-called Clear Grits,[33] with the radical, antibusiness, anticlerical Parti Rouge of Quebec. Denied victory at the national level, the Liberals concentrated their efforts on the provinces, and by the time they came to power in 1896 they controlled the government of every province but Quebec. In that province, Wilfred Laurier, the future national leader and Prime Minister, had been engaged during the 1880s and early 1890s in broadening the base of Liberal support by transforming the Rouges into a moderate reform party that was at the same time palatable to the Catholic Church hierarchy and the traditional doctor-lawyer elites of the small towns.[34]

The growth of grassroots Liberal provincial support brought a corresponding slow decline in Conservative fortunes. The original biethnic coalition manufactured by John A. Macdonald and Etienne Cartier was severely strained by the hanging of the French-Catholic half-breed Louis Riel following the Northwest Rebellion in 1885.[35] It was further exacerbated by the popularity of the anti-Catholic Equal Rights Association and, finally, was dissolved in 1896 by the ethnic–religious controversy surrounding the issue of state supported Catholic schools in Manitoba (the Manitoba School Question).

A national convention modeled on the American conventions chose Laurier as the Liberal leader in 1893. A combination of his own political skills, economic prosperity, and the chauvanism generated by the inclusion in the federal union of the new western provinces of Saskatchewan and Alberta kept his Liberal Administration in office from 1896–1911. His downfall is usually ascribed to the alienation of isolationist elements[36] within his own province. This was the result of a Government proposal to begin building a Canadian Navy. The loss of important business support in Ontario because they had championed limited reciprocal free trade with the United States also was costly to the Laurier Government.

The alliance between Quebec nationalism and Ontario anti-Americanism that brought the Conservatives under Robert Borden to power[37] dissolved during the Conscription Crisis of 1917. The bitterness of French Canada toward the Conservatives was not allayed when Borden retired, and Arthur Meighen, the very symbol of Conscription to many French Canadians, became Prime Minister in 1920. One manifestation of the attitude in Quebec was the failure of the Conservatives to win a single seat in the national election of 1921. However, Quebec was not the only province in which the Conservatives fared poorly in 1921. They also failed to win a seat in the three prairie provinces of Manitoba, Saskatchewan, and Alberta. Nor did the Liberals enjoy outstanding success on the prairies; they were able to elect only two members while thirty-eight of the prairie seats went to candidates of the newly formed Progressive party.

According to the historian William Morton,[38] the Progressive party "was a revolt against a concept of Canadian economic policy and of Canadian political practice." In their view, a rural agricultural West was being thoroughly and ruthlessly exploited in the best colonial tradition by the financial and industrial elite of the urban East. The two political parties functioned as a kind of "executive arm" of this elite. The Eastern majority in the parliamentary caucuses was employed both to articulate the interests of the exploiters and to throttle the protests of the oppressed. The Progressive party revolt, then, was as much a revolt against disciplined party government as it was against the economic policies articulated by the parties.

Although the Progressive party was moribund by 1925 and dead as a political force after the 1926 national election, William Morton[39] feels it had the following consequences for Canadian politics: (1) Canada changed from a two-party to a multiparty system with the emergence from the Progressives of the Social Credit and Cooperative Commonwealth Federation (CCF) parties; (2) the strength of party identification in the Canadian electorate was weakened; and (3) party discipline in the Canadian House of Commons became less stringent (in particular, the bonds of caucus became weaker).

The first of the two new parties to arise out of the Progressive movement was the Social Credit party. Under the leadership of William "Bible Bill" Aberhart, it was able to parlay strong support from former Progressives and from members of the United Farmers of Alberta into victory in the Alberta provincial election of 1935. John Irving[40] explained the early success of Social Credit party in Alberta in terms of four factors: the social context (widespread depression and social disorganization); the desire for meaning in a chaotic and fluid environment; the satisfaction of psychological and physical needs; and proper conditions of suggestability (an unsophisticated electorate bombarded with appropriate slogans and symbols).

By the end of the depression the party was so well entrenched as to be virtually unopposed in the legislature. Since 1952 it also has formed the government in British Columbia. Despite this regional success at the provincial level, the party made virtually no headway nationally until Real Caouette,[41] a small town car dealer, led twenty-six Quebec Creditistes into the House of Commons in 1962. For approximately a year he appeared weekly on television to reiterate such themes as poverty in the midst of plenty, prosperity through the creation of social credit, the corruption and moral bankruptcy of the two old parties, and the failure of the two old parties to either offer a meaningful choice or to articulate the interests of the people.

This revival of slogans and doctrine which initially had helped make Social Credit successful in the West was somewhat ironic as the Western party leaders had for some time ceased to pay more than periodic lip service to them. Instead, they emphasized the stability and success of their provincial regimes and, at the national level, Ernest Manning and Robert Thompson called upon Conservatives to join with them in a new and real conservative coalition which could successfully oppose the now-socialist Liberal party.

By the same token, the initial intention of the CCF was to eradicate the capitalist economic system and to establish a socialist society: this was modified[42] as the party sought to broaden the base of its electoral support and to encourage middle-class participation in organizational activity. Like the Social Credit, the CCF experienced initial success in the West and, in fact, was able to generate sufficient support among rural voters in Saskatchewan,[43] to gain control of the provincial government in 1944, and to maintain that control for approximately twenty years. During the war years their popularity spread to Ontario in the east and to British Columbia in the west, and by war's end there were high hopes among party leaders that they might supplant the Conservatives as the Official Opposition to the Liberals in the House of Commons. These hopes were never realized, the party never having elected more than twenty-eight MPs to any House of Commons. In 1961, the close ties between the CCF and organized Canadian labor were formalized, and from this marriage emerged the current New Democratic Party (NDP). To date, the only fruit of this union has been the marked increase in support the NDP has received in metropolitan areas. However, they have been able to console themselves with the belief that they pushed a series of reluctant Liberal Administrations into passing the bulk of the welfare legislation enjoyed by Canadians. The extent to which the Liberals had to be pushed, however, is a matter of debate.

The party had come under the leadership of the remarkable William Lyon Mackenzie King in 1919.[44] In 1921 he became the Prime Minister of a minority Liberal Government and, except for a brief period in 1925 and the years 1930–1935, remained the leader of both party and country until his resignation and replacement by Louis St. Laurent in 1948. King's perception of a political party was that it was primarily a mechanism for mediating and resolving intergroup conflicts rather than generating policy proposals. Thus, R. M. Dawson[45] wrote of him, "He considered that the parties in Canada had two major functions: the propagation and carrying out of ideas and policies, and the bringing together of diverse and even conflicting groups and interests so as to secure a working agreement and a measure of common action. The second function was in his eyes even more important than the first."

Accordingly, his early years in office were given over to wooing the Progressives back into the Liberal fold. That he was successful in his task is suggested by the fact that the Liberals won 47 percent of the parliamentary seats in the prairie provinces of Manitoba, Saskatchewan, and Alberta in the five national elections from 1926 to 1945, despite the fact that this area was the base of both the CCF and Social Credit party strength. Even more important was his success with French-Canadian voters in Quebec. The party won no fewer than 89 percent of Quebec's parliamentary seats during the 1926–1945 period. It was King who revived Macdonald's idea of a French-Canadian "first lieutenant." As Quebec members supposedly were interested in patronage, French-Canadian MPs generally were appointed to such "pork-barrel" Cabinet positions as Post Office, Public Works, and Justice.[46]

Despite his supposed preference for the honest broker role, and his reluctance to initiate policy proposals that might generate conflict, the foundation of much of Canada's welfare program was laid during his tenure of office. This program, together with proposals intended to broaden the industrial base of the Canadian economy, were pursued by King's successors during the years 1948–1957. In one respect, it was the insistence of the Liberals (particularly, C. D. Howe) on pursuing what was in their view an essential if unpopular industrial policy that led to the famous Pipline Debate, and their subsequent defeat in the election of June 1957.

In that year, John Diefenbaker,[47] a small-town Saskatchewan lawyer, who had only recently (1956) been chosen leader of his party, led the Conservatives to a close victory, and from his colleagues formed a minority government. The next year, largely as a result of his personal charisma, the Conservatives won the greatest electoral victory in Canadian history. During that campaign, Diefenbaker[48] struck first a spark and then a fire in the electorate with his famous "vision." Parliamentary correspondent Arthur Blakely,[48] paraphrasing the Conservative leader's oratory, described it as

> a vision of Canada's future. A great future. A future which is all bound up with Canada's great northland and its untapped riches. It is a vision which contemplates . . . the building of dams, the establishment of great new cities, the creation of great new wealth. And all of this in our generation. Oh, yes, he admits, with a fine scorn, there are the scoffers, the cynics, the unbelievers. Those who suggest, among other things, that roads in the north will run "from igloo to igloo." But those imaginative Canadians, . . . those who make this a land flowing in milk and honey in our own time, they will have a chance to deal with the scoffers on March 31.

Although the Conservatives suffered so sharp a reversal in fortunes in 1962 that they were again reduced to forming a minority government, they nevertheless have generated some important changes in the nature of party representation in Parliament. First, their party which for so many years was dependent on urban Ontario for its electoral support[49] and was anathema to prairie voters, now draws its sustenance principally from the latter region.[50] Second, the Liberals who for years and with justification claimed to be Canada's only "national" party can no longer make that claim, as they were virtually wiped out by the Conservatives in the four Western Provinces during the period 1957–1962.[51] In addition, their parliamentary strength was sharply reduced in the four Maritime Provinces.[52] Third, the Conservatives and not the NDP are now the party of the prairie farmer. The NDP electoral support since 1957 increasingly has come from urban Ontario, Manitoba, and British Columbia. Fourth, the undisputed hegemony which the Liberals enjoyed in Quebec national politics was disrupted by the Conservatives in 1958. Although the fortune of the Conservatives again has declined in Quebec, a substantial other-than-Liberal vote has persisted.[53]

The dimensions underlying the Canadian party struggle are suggested even by this very brief summary. As Canada grew to include the provinces not encompassed by the union of 1867, the cultural and economic cleavages generated by the existence of a large, homogeneous, relatively unassimilated French-Catholic minority in the midst of an English-Protestant majority, together with a populous urban industrial region centered in what was essentially an underpopulated rural and agricultural society, encouraged strong cultural and economic regionalism. In turn, the meeting of these regional needs by the legislative representatives from these areas was made particularly difficult by the British model parliamentary system with its requirement that members of the legislative parties act cohesively. The two new national parties which then developed experienced limited success nationally, but were able to capture and hold office in three of the four Western Provinces. The cleavages (at least the economic ones) have blurred and, indeed, there appears to have been a convergence between the NDP and the Liberal parties. The NDP, despite the fact that it began as a socialist sect dedicated to the eradication of capitalism and the establishment of a new social order, has lost much of its ideological zeal,[54] while the Liberal party, presumably under pressure from the NDP, has moved left.

On the other end of the continuum, the western wing of the Social Credit party increasingly has become conservative. From its inception, Social Credit leaders had stressed the fact that they were a reform rather than a revolutionary party, and that their "funny money" and other financial panaceas were intended to make capitalism work rather than to destroy it. With continued electoral success in Alberta and British Columbia, these slogans were soft-pedaled and largely forgotten.

As for the Conservatives, undoubtedly they have moved somewhat to the left under the leadership of Diefenbaker; but their popular image and policy preferences, as exemplified by the ideological positions of our Conservative respondents on selected policy issues, are those of a group most at home on the right of the political continuum.

Despite the apparent ideological convergence of the two parties on the left and, to a lesser extent, the two on the right, the four have continued to maintain their separate existences. Coupled with the fact that since 1957 neither the Conservatives nor the Liberals have been able to receive consistent massive support from Quebec, the result has been a period of minority government (in four of the five national elections the winning party has failed to elect a majority of its candidates to the House of Commons). Historically, the long periods of national dominance enjoyed first by the Conservatives and then by the Liberals were predicated on the receipt of overwhelming support from the Quebec electorate. One reason why this support was so readily forthcoming already has been suggested—the elevation of French Canadians to highly visible leadership positions. According to some students of Canadian politics, however, several more basic reasons explain why for so many years Quebec served as a French-Canadian equivalent of the American Solid South. Indeed, a rather elaborate theory posits that French-Canadian political behavior is largely a function of subcultural influences in Quebec. We are interested in this cultural theory because it has implications for legislative behavior and because the cleavage between French Canadians and English Canadians has been regarded as the most important and enduring in Canadian society.[55]

### *A Cultural Theory of French-Canadian Political Behavior*

Very briefly, the basic assumption underlying the theory is that French Canadians neither have understood nor really believed in democratic institutions and processes. Rather, they only have made use of some of these institutions (notably political parties and legislatures) to insure their survival as a distinct ethnic-religious group (*la survivance*). Thus Arthur Maheux[56] claims that in this century continuous emphasis has been placed on the peculiar "mission" or "vocation" of the French Canadian, and on the necessity for maintaining a French and Catholic culture. Such a culture has not been oriented toward democratic institutions and values:

> The attitudes toward democracy of the two main groups are not quite and can hardly be the same. . . . If we ask a French Canadian what are the elements of the French heritage he will list, in the following order, religion, philosophy, language, literature, history, fine arts, economics, law and government. An English Canadian lists the same elements but he will put them in a different order: for him the first items are the government and economics and by government he means democracy. That difference should not be slighted, it is of real importance in the daily life of the Canadian nation. If both groups disagree about the value and the working of democratic institutions, they are bound to clash, sometimes bitterly.

According to Hubert Guindon,[57] the Roman Catholic Church has had a disproportionately powerful and unhappy influence on both the social and political life of Quebec:

> The clergy controlled the avenue of social promotion by its control of the educational structure. It socialized in tender youth all the budding professionals and politicans. So if they enacted the political rules of the game, most of the script was clerically censored and the actors were clerically rehearsed and directed.

Probably the harshest criticism of French-Canadian attitudes toward democracy is that of Pierre Elliot Trudeau,[58] law professor and Member of Parliament:

> In the opinion of the French in Canada, government of the people, by the people, could not be for the people, but merely for the English speaking part of the people. So they believed and so they could only *make believe*

> in democracy . . . In all important aspects of national politics, guile, compromise and a subtle kind of blackmail decided their course and determined their allegiance. If I were to quote all the material proving that French-Canadians fundamentally do not believe in democracy, and that on the whole neither pulpit, nor legislature, nor the radio, nor the press is doing much to instill such a belief, I would encroach upon eternity.

In turn these attitudes toward democratic institutions and processes presumably affect the quality of French-Canadian elected officials, their motives for becoming candidates, and their subsequent behavior as legislators. For example, one French-Canadian parliamentary leader said:[59]

> You must understand that the average French-Canadian looks at politics strictly in terms of what politics can give him personally. He is not concerned with the general well-being of the community or the larger public good, but what is in it for him. This has had its effect on the type of people who run for office in Quebec. They cannot be called first-class people, certainly. They are people who are going to do things for individuals they feel will get them elected. They aren't concerned with policy but with doing the necessary little jobs so that enough people will elect them. We are elected by the people as delegates. They elect those people whom they feel will best represent their individual personal interests. The direction the party moves and the policies it adopts, these are of little consequence to most French-Canadian MPs. He is interested in one thing only—getting re-elected—and so the things he concerns himself with are those things that will help him personally and that he can put to his own political advantage.

Another MP claimed:[60]

> There are primarily two reasons why a person goes into politics (in Quebec): The first is it will help him personally, financially. You know, it will help his law business or insurance or something else he is in. Second, if he already has money then it will provide him with social prestige. Oh, how some of them love the MP after their name! It means something in their communities, they're looked up to. The really ambitious younger ones of course hope to do even better—to become Ministers if we win the Government. . . .
>
> When he's here all he's interested in is getting re-elected. You have only to look at the party's national conventions. Where do you find the French? Not in the policy-making groups but in those pertaining to party organization. This is what they are interested in because organization is what gets you elected! . . .
>
> We are always trying to represent the interests of Quebec. You see we are a minority group but an extremely powerful and organized one. As their representatives we tend to look at and are only interested in things if they affect Quebec. We fight our national elections, in spite of what you may have heard, on Quebec and not national problems. We are elected by the people as delegates. As long as we can get things for the constituency, or, best of all, look after individual problems, then we are content to let the English run the party!

According to the culturalists, the norms of groups such as the Catholic Church and its educational institutions are so widely shared in Quebec, and they have been so completely internalized that they predispose legislators acculturated in that milieu to behave in a fashion different from Canadian legislators subjected to other subcultural influences. Specifically, the French Canadian is motivated to undertake political activity by status or by economic aspirations or both; his goals as legislator are narrow, concrete, and oriented toward his district; his representational style is that of a delegate; and his chief concern is not with the nation or national problems but with performing services for constituents as such activity is most likely to re-elect him. By implication, legislators who are not French Canadians, as they have internalized different norms, are motivated by other than status or economic considerations: their goals are broad, relatively abstract, and oriented toward the nation; their representational style is that of trustee; and their principal concern is the nation or the innovation of national policies or both. In Chapters 4, 5, and 6 this extreme cultural theory of legislative behavior will be tested by creating an ideal French Canadian, and determining the degree of "fit" between the data on French-Canadian motives, goals, and representational role perceptions and the above theoretical expectations. The alternative notion that the behavior of legislators is a product of expectations derived from experiences prior to incumbency and perspectives developed subsequently also will be subjected to analysis.

## *SUMMARY*

In this section, the Canadian parliamentary system has been examined in terms of certain properties and attributes. The Constitution of 1867 allocated very substantial powers to the national Parliament. In Canada, the Parliament consists of a Governor-General, an appointed Senate, and a popularly elected House of Commons from which is drawn the real executive. The Government, or the Administration, prepares the bulk of the legislative program which the House of Commons considers during a parliamentary session. In this sense, it integrates the work of both governing and opposition party members.

A position in the Administration affords an opportunity to specialize to a limited number of members of the governing party. Leaders of the opposition parties also must acquire special knowledge, and develop some *expertise* in those areas in which they criticize the Government. However, the majority of the members of a Canadian House of Commons apparently do not acquire expert knowledge in substantive areas for which legislation is intended. A committee system, which in other Western legislatures affords individuals such an opportunity, performs largely educative and cathartic functions in Canada.

Parliamentary procedure is intended to regulate interpersonal behavior and to facilitate the passage of the Government's legislative program. Because of the relative inexperience of most legislators, and the large turnover following a national election, there is some doubt as to how visible and, consequently, how effective are current procedural norms.

Although there is only a very limited opportunity for back bench MPs to initiate legislation, there are three institutionalized opportunities for them to participate in policy evaluations. These come at the beginning of a parliamentary session in the debate of the Speech from the Throne, during the debates on estimates, and on the budget proposals. Members also can satisfy the need to participate meaningfully in the deliberation of the Common in the daily question period. A very brief history of the national parties and a description of a cultural theory of French-Canadian political behavior conclude this chapter.

## Notes

1. For an excellent annotated bibliography of relevant Canadian scholarship, particularly historical, see R. M. Dawson and Norman Ward, *The Government of Canada,* 4th ed. (Toronto: University of Toronto Press, 1963), pp. 583–588.

2. The Governor-General in Council (the Cabinet) was given the power to disallow offensive provincial legislation. As this power could destroy a federal system, it has been used very sparingly.

3. The Cabinet is not mentioned in the Constitution. The only oblique reference to it is contained in Section XI wherein it is stated that "there shall be a Council to aid and advise in the Government of Canada, to be styled the Queen's Privy Council for Canada, and the persons who are to be Members of that Council shall be from time to time chosen and summoned by the Governor General. . . ." All Cabinet Ministers are appointed to the Privy Council, and at any time the Council consists of all living individuals who at some time have been appointed thereto. In practice, only current Cabinet members are summoned to meetings of the Council.

4. See the discussion by Dawson and Ward, pp. 181–185.

5. As the possession of specialized knowledge is an asset that may facilitate appointment to an Administration, in a limited sense, *all* would-be ministers or parliamentary assistants are afforded some motive to specialize.

6. Dawson and Ward, p. 226.

7. *Parliamentary Debates on the Subject of the Confederation of the British North American Provinces* (Quebec: 1865), p. 35. Quoted in Robert A. Mackay, *The Unreformed Senate of Canada* (rev. ed.), The Carleton Library, No. 6 (Toronto: McClelland and Stewart Ltd., 1963), p. 49.

8. J. A. Macdonald, "Notes on the Quebec Conference, 1864," in A. G. Doughty (ed.), *The Canadian Historical Review,* **1** (1920), 31.

9. Robert A. Mackay, *The Unreformed Senate of Canada* (rev. ed.), The Carleton Library, No. 6 (Toronto: McClelland and Stewart Ltd., 1963), pp. 88 and 95.

10. See F. A. Kunz, *The Modern Senate of Canada, 1925–1963: A Re-Appraisal* (Toronto: The University of Toronto Press, 1965), particularly pp. 311–315, and Henry S. Albinski, "The Canadian Senate: Politics and the Constitution," *The American Political Science Review,* **57** (1963), 378–391. Specifically, the Senate in 1961 prevented the adoption of a bill that permitted the Minister of Finance to significantly alter tariffs without the necessity of public notice. That same

year the Senate also would not agree to a Cabinet-sponsored bill providing for the removal of the Governor of the Bank of Canada.

11. Kunz, pp. 74–75.

12. Dawson and Ward, p. 345. The data for our sample of the 1962 House shows a turnover of 39 percent in membership from the previous Parliament.

13. John Porter, "Political Parties and the Political Career," *Canadian Forum,* **38** (1958), 27–54.

14. This is a nonparametric statistic proposed by Leo. A. Goodman and William H. Kruskal, "Measure of Association for Cross-Classification," *Journal of the American Statistical Association,* **44** (1954), 732–764. Although less frequently employed in analyses of essentially ordinal data than the Tau Beta correlation, the Gamma, unlike the Beta, is not subject to a "square table" requirement (tables are two by two or three by three and so forth).

Generally, correlations of 0.20 are reported in this analysis.

15. Halifax, Nova Scotia, and Queens, Prince Edward Island are two-member constituencies.

16. The 28th Parliament will be the first elected under the latest reapportionment of the country.

17. There are a number of exceptions to this rule that we will not detail.

18. Closure was first introduced into Canadian parliamentary procedure in 1913. Under closure the Cabinet Minister, providing he has given notice of his intention at an earlier sitting, may move that further consideration of a question be not further postponed. The motion is not debatable and, if carried, no person can speak for more than twenty minutes on the question to which the closure has been applied. It is a drastic and rarely used device that is likely to become an issue in the next general election. The threat of closure ordinarily is sufficient warning to opposition members that the Government will take a firm stand and that some accommodation must be reached to bring debate on an issue to an end.

The "previous question" permits a member at any time during a debate to move that the "question be now put." The motion is debatable, but no amendment to it or to the main motion is permitted. The motion must be put to a vote immediately after the conclusion of the debate on the motion of the "previous question."

19. See Allan Kornberg, "The Rules of the Game in the Canadian House of Commons," *Journal of Politics,* **26** (1964), 363–366.

20. Former Prime Minister John Diefenbaker's attempts to establish a permanent Speakership in 1957 are said to have floundered when his informal choice for Speaker, Stanley Knowles (NDP), would not agree to serve in that capacity.

21. The bitterness and frequent unruliness generated by the 26th Parliament's debates over a new flag, the "repatriation" of the Constitution, and the alleged immorality of the Liberal Government, probably encouraged party leaders to retain provisional Standing Order 12, adopted June 11, 1965, for the 27th Parliament. Order 12.1 states:

> Mr. Speaker shall preserve order and decorum, and shall decide questions of order. In explaining a point of order or practice, he shall state the Standing Order or practice applicable to the case. No debate shall be permitted on any such decision, nor shall any such decision be subject to an appeal to the House.

The Special Committee on Procedure recommended that the Provisional Standing Order be retained during the next (28th) Parliament. Thus, it now appears that this provisional increase in the Speaker's powers will become permanent.

22. Although questions primarily are asked to embarrass the Government, at times they have helped bring to light and rectify administrative abuses of the public.

23. Since 1957, the Chairman of the Committee on Public Accounts, the financial watchdog of the House, has been chosen from an opposition party.

24. Dawson and Ward, pp. 380–381.

25. Dawson and Ward, p. 382.

26. In contrast, several solid studies of the committee system of the American Congress are available. See, for example, Nicholas A. Masters, "Committee Assignments in the House of Representatives," *American Political Science Review,* **55** (1961), 345–357; George Goodwin, Jr., "Subcommittees: The Miniature Legislatures of Congress," *American Political Science Review,* **56** (1962), 596–604; Robert L. Peabody, "The Enlarged Rules Committee" in Robert L. Peabody and Nelson W. Polsby (eds.), *New Perspectives on the House of Representatives* (Chicago, Ill.: Rand McNally & Company, 1963), pp. 129–164; James Cochrane, "Partisan Aspects of Congressional Committee Staffing," *Western Political Quarterly,* **17** (1964), 338–348.

27. However, it should be noted that a study by Stanley V. Vardys of nine of the thirty-four select committees in the 80th to 85th Congresses suggested that such select committees do not influence congressional decision-making, although they do provide a public forum for various group interests and also perform a valuable educative function, not only for their own members and other Congressmen (as is the case with select committee in the Canadian system), but also, for a variety of constituency groups. See S. V. Vardys, "Select Committees of the House of Representative," *Midwest Journal of Political Science,* **6** (1962), 247–265.

28. John Meisel, "The Formulation of Liberal and Conservative Programmes in the 1957 Canadian General Election," *Canadian Journal of Economics and Political Science,* **26** (1960), 565–574. See also J. E. Hodgetts, "The Liberal and the Bureaucrat," *Queens Quarterly,* **62** (1955), 176–183.

29. Allan Kornberg, "Caucus and Cohesion in Canadian Parliamentary Parties," *American Political Science Review,* **60** (March 1966), 84.

30. The single best treatment of the origins of Canadian parties probably is Escott M. Reid, "The Rise of National Parties in Canada," *Papers and Proceedings of the Canadian Political Science Association,* **4** (1932), 187–200. For an excellent bibliography of the available literature on Canadian parties, see Hugh Thorburn (ed.), *Party Politics in Canada,* (Toronto: Prentice-Hall of Canada, 1963), pp. 168–172.

31. See Donald Creighton's two-volume work on John A. Macdonald, *The Young Politician* and *The Old Chieftain* (Toronto: The Macmillan Co. of Canada, Ltd., (1952).

32. Athough Macdonald himself was more moderate, their spokesman, Sir Etienne Cartier, became Macdonald's first lieutenant. See John I. Cooper, "The Political Ideas of George Etienne Cartier," *Canadian Historical Review,* **23** (1942), 286–294.

33. For a biography of a founding father of Canadian Liberalism, see Dale C. Thomson, *Alexander McKenzie: Clear Grit,* (Toronto: The Macmillan Co. of Canada, Ltd., 1960).

34. An interesting biography of Laurier is provided by Joseph Schull, *Laurier* (Toronto: The Macmillan Co. of Canada, Ltd., 1966).

35. According to John W. Dafoe, the veteran editor of the Winnipeg Free

Press and a long-time student of Canadian politics, the execution of Riel changed the whole course of Canadian politics, in that it destroyed the position of the Conservatives in the most conservative Canadian province, Quebec. See his *Laurier: A Study in Canadian Polities* (Toronto: The T. Allen Co., 1922).

36. As a portent of events to come during World War I and II, the editorials of the influential *Le Devoir* claimed that Laurier's navy would conscript French-Canadian boys "to maintain at the price of their blood, the supremacy of the British flag in Asia or Africa." Quoted in Bruce Hutchison, *Mr. Prime Minister: 1867–1964,* (Toronto: Longmans Canada, Ltd., 1964), p. 139.

37. Certain elements in the Conservative party periodically have manifested the Anti-Americanism which was an important pre-condition of Canadian existence. In the elections of 1930, 1957, and 1963 the Canadian-American relationship was an extremely important issue which was very successfully exploited by many Conservative candidates.

38. William Morton, *The Progressive Party in Canada* (Toronto: University of Toronto Press, 1963), p. 288.

39. In Chapter 6 we will present data that suggest that the strength of party identification indeed has been weakened in Canada. The data in Chapter 7 support Morton's claim that the bonds of caucus do not bind individuals too tightly, even in a parliamentary system of the British model.

40. John Irving, *The Social Credit Movement in Alberta* (Toronto: University of Toronto Press, 1959).

41. During the 26th Parliament, Mr. Caouette and eleven other Social Credit MPs from Quebec split with party leader Robert Thompson and formed a new party, Le Ralliement des Creditistes. During this Parliament two other Social Creditors left their party and joined the Conservative caucus.

42. In their 1956 Winnipeg Declaration, the party expressed their willingness to tolerate a "mixed" planned–free enterprise economy.

43. See Seymour M. Lipset, *Agrarian Socialism* (Berkeley, Calif.: University of California Press, 1950).

44. For a description of King's career in Parliament prior to his selection as Liberal leader, see F. A. McGregor, *The Fall and Rise of Mackenzie King: 1911–1919*, (Toronto: The MacMillan Co. of Canada, Ltd., 1962).

45. R. MacGregor Dawson, *William Lyon Mackenzie King: A Political Biography* (Toronto: University of Toronto Press, 1958), p. 319. Beck and Dooley perceived King only in the role of "broker." According to them, "In King's view a Canadian political leader could not be doctrinaire; he had to balance one pressure group against another, and he had to prevent issues becoming so clearly defined that they caused deep divisions," J. M. Beck and D. J. Dooley, "Party Images in Canada," *Queen's Quarterly,* 67 (196), 437.

46. King's practices were bitterly resented by many members of Quebec's intellectual and academic communities. One such individual, himself a Quebec Liberal MP, said during an interview in 1962; "Are you familiar with Laurendeau's Cannibal King thesis—the way the English used to deal with the Negro in Africa through his leader, a Cannibal King? Well, that is how King dealt with Quebec." Another said:

> Our English speaking colleagues tend to think of us as a group. Quebec must have a voice in this or a share in that. They separate us, lump us together in a group. A party must obtain a majority of the seats and votes in Quebec to win and they are willing to pay for those votes with a bone. In return for patronage, providing services for our constituents, it is understood that

they will control the policies of the party. They act as if only *they* had the right to decide the policies the party is to advocate. They take it for granted that they have the right to govern—with a French front man of course—a Lapointe, a St. Laurent, a Chevrier, who are to keep Quebec in line in return for the bone they throw us. . . . They give us our little symbols, they let us talk and argue about nationalism, a Canadian flag, a national anthem—all window-dressing! The real decisions are made by them!

47. For an interesting albeit biased description of Mr. Diefenbaker's tenure as Prime Minister, see Peter C. Newman, *Renegade in Power: The Diefenbaker Years* (Toronto: McClelland and Stewart, Ltd., 1963).

48. Arthur Blakely, *Montreal Gazette* (March 26, 1958).

49. Lionel H. Laing, "The Patterns of Canadian Politics: The Election of 1945," *American Political Science Review,* **40** (1946), 760–765. Laing showed that in both the 1940 and 1945 elections approximately two-thirds of the Conservative MPs were able to win elections in constituencies within a radius of eighty-seven miles from Toronto, Ontario.

50. From 1926 to 1953 the Conservatives won only 12 percent of the seats from the three prairie provinces whereas from 1957 to 1962, they were victorious in 71 percent of these contests. In the 1963 and 1965 elections, held since the study was completed, the Conservatives have raised their proportion of victories in the prairies to 86 percent.

51. From 1926 to 1953 the Liberals won 45 percent of the parliamentary seats in the four Western Provinces. From 1957 to 1962, this proportion dropped to less than 7 percent, and has risen to only 12 percent in the last two national elections (1963 and 1965).

52. From 1926 to 1953 the Liberals captured 64 percent of the seats in the Maritime Provinces. This was reduced to 34 percent during the years 1957–1962, but has risen to 48 percent in the two elections.

53. Since 1958, the Liberals have been able to capture only 44 percent of the Quebec votes, while during the period 1926–1957 they had the support of 58 percent of the Quebec electorate.

54. Leo Zakuta, "The CCF–NDP: Membership in a Becalmed Protest Movement," *Party Politics in Canada* (ed.), Hugh Thorburn (Toronto: Prentice-Hall of Canada, 1963), pp. 96–108.

55. For example, Leon D. Epstein feels that this cleavage is more significant than any equivalent division in the United States, and that Canada, unless it is fragmented by a successful separatist movement in Quebec, is irrevocably biethnic. See Leon D. Epstein, "A Comparative Study of Canadian Parties," *American Political Science Review,* **58** (1964), 46–59.

56. Arthur Maheux, "Democracy and the French Canadian," in Douglas Grant, *Quebec Today* (Toronto: University of Toronto Press, 1958), pp. 341–342.

57. Hubert Guindon, "The Social Evolution of Quebec Reconsidered," *Canadian Journal of Economics and Political Science,* **26** (1960), 545.

58. Pierre Elliot Trudeau, "Some Obstacles to Democracy in Quebec," *Canadian Journal of Economics and Political Science,* **24** (1958), 297–314.

59. Personal interview (Ottawa, November 1962).

60. Personal interview (Ottawa, November 1962).

# 3

# The House of Commons of the 25th Parliament

Recent systematic studies of the social backgrounds of political decision-makers have rather effectively undermined the log-cabin-to-Congress or, for that matter, the poverty-to-Parliament conception of legislative leadership. The romantic notion, stemming from the Jacksonian era in American politics, that members of democratic representative assemblies mirror the social characteristics of the constituents they represent, largely has been invalidated by the revelation that legislative bodies are elite groups which are highly atypical of their societies. Generally, such studies have accomplished this by comparing certain characteristics of the legislators (education, occupation, social background, ethnicity, religion) with those of a cross section of their electorate either longitudinally or for a particular period of time.

The collection of such data is motivated by an assumption, not always made specific, that *who legislators are* affects the product generated by the systems of which they are a part.[1] That is, the skill patterns, the values, and the attitudes that they bring to the legislature affect their subsequent performances as legislators, particularly their interactions with significant others who are within or who make demands upon the legislative system. Longitudinal studies presumably have the additional merits of revealing the shifting power bases of a particular society, and the subcultural and organizational screening devices employed in leadership recruitment.

In this chapter, the occupations and educational attainments of the legislators in the present sample are compared with a sample of American Congressmen, candidates for the British House of Commons, and with a cross section of the Canadian population. Next to be considered are the patterns of political socialization insofar as that phenomenon is measured by an interest in the political process. Attention is given to the manner in which political interest is related to individual backgrounds and to the respondents' perceptions of their initial recruitment for the political system. Finally, there is a description of their experience as public and party officeholders prior to election to parliament, and a delineation of future expectations. There will be suggestions as to how variations in individual background are likely to affect the perception and performance of legislative roles in the Canadian Parliament, and suggestions as to how certain societal and organizational variables interact in the process of legislative recruitment.

## SOCIAL BACKGROUND

Canadian MPs, like their counterparts in other Western democracies, tend to be members of a profession, usually law.[2] Although they constitute only a fraction of one percent of the population, lawyers made up fully 33 percent of the sample.[3] In contrast, Austin Ranney[4] found that only 15 percent of the nonincumbent candidates for the British House of Commons during the years 1951–1964 were barristers and solicitors. Alexander Brady,[5] in an insightful essay, suggests why this disparity should exist. He argues that the legal profession always has been more important in the Canadian than the British House of Commons because Canada, unlike Britain, has never had a governing class with the leisure, interest, or skills required for high public office. Lawyers have been a substitute because they have the requisite skills and because they, better than any other occupational group, are able to combine politics and a profession. Thus, nine of Canada's thirteen Prime Ministers have been lawyers, and about one-third of the membership of any House are lawyers.[6] As was indicated above, the data for this particular sample support Brady's estimate of the proportion of members who are lawyers. Other data, gleaned from the *Report of the Chief Electoral Officer,* suggest that the parties, although they may vary in their ability or desire to recruit lawyers, all find lawyers generally make attractive or winning candidates. Normally, the percentage of a party's winners who are lawyers exceeds the proportion of lawyers who are candidates. Thus, in the 165 sample constituencies, it was found that 32 percent of all Liberal, 26 percent of all Conservative, 5 percent of all New Democrat, and 2 percent of all Social Credit candidates in eight national elections during the period 1945–1965 were members of the legal profession. However, fully 40 percent of the Liberal, 29 percent of the Conservative, 7 percent of the New Democrat and 4 percent of the Social Credit winners for that period were also lawyers.

Businessmen, both self-employed and corporate executives, were overrepresented in the House. Taken together, 76 percent of the sample were in business or members of the professions, while only 18 percent of the Canadian working population (ages 25–64) of 1961 were so employed.[7] As one would suspect from their occupations, they were also an extraordinarily well-educated group[8] and, in fact, compared favorably in terms of education and prestigious occupations with both American Senators and candidates for the British House of Commons (see Table 3.1).

Another indication of the elite status of Canadian MPs is afforded by the use of a scoring system that permits occupation to be treated as a linear and continuous variable in statistical analysis.[9] The two-digit scores estimated by Otis Duncan[10] range from 00 to 96 and are a composite of information on occupation, educational attainment, and prestige ascribed to the several occupations. They provide a convenient and reliable measure of socioeconomic status (SES).

The SES scores of the four parties' candidates in six national elections (165 sample constituencies) indicate that: (1) a "status gap" exists between the candidates of the major and minor parties; (2) with the exception of the Social Credit party, the status of candidates varies with the ethnic composition of the regions from which they are drawn; (3) candidates for the parliaments of the post World War II era tend to be drawn from the upper occupational and education strata of Canadian society (see Table 3.2).

In part, a superior education and occupation are a function of relatively high class origin. Not surprisingly, 16 percent of the 1962 sample of MPs had fathers who were members of a profession. In 1921, when the majority of their fathers would have been living and working, only 6 percent of the Canadian population were practicing a profession. Still, the social origins of this group of legislators were humbler than a sample of American Senators[11] and, unlike the Americans, they did not overrepresent the Anglo-Saxon Protestant elements of their society.[12] In fact, their ethnic and religious backgrounds reflected, fairly accurately, the distribution of these characteristics in the Canadian population (see Table 3.3).

TABLE 3.1 PRINCIPAL OCCUPATIONS[a] AND LEVEL OF EDUCATION OF CANADIAN MPs, AMERICAN SENATORS, AND CANDIDATES FOR THE BRITISH HOUSE OF COMMONS[b] (percentage)

| | *Canadian MPs* | *American Senators* | *Candidates for British MP* |
|---|---|---|---|
| Occupation | | | |
| Professionals | 51 | 64 | 45 |
| Proprietor–managers | 25 | 29 | 20 |
| Farmers | 12 | 7 | 4 |
| Low status | 12 | | 22 |
| Other | | | 9 |
| | (*N* = 165) | (*N* = 180) | (*N* = 2742) |
| Education | | | |
| College or university | 72 | 85 | 52 |
| Less than college or university | 28 | 15 | 48 |
| | | | (*N* = 3182)[c] |

[a] In the classification of occupations, "farmers" refers to farm owners; "low status" occupations are blue and white collar workers such as laborers, truckdrivers, plumbers, clerks, typists, salesmen, and so forth.

[b] Data on the candidates for the British House of Commons are derived from Austin Ranney, *Pathways to Parliament* (Madison, Wis.: University of Wisconsin Press, 1965). The figures on occupation are for Conservative and Labor party candidates only. Ranney's categories have been juggled somewhat to make them approximate Matthews' and our own classifications. Thus, "farmers" have been removed from his proprietor-managerial classes, "teachers" have been included among his professionals, and "low status" for the British sample refers only to manual workers and white collar individuals. His candidates do not include incumbents of the House during the period 1951–1964.

[c] The data on education include an additional 440 Liberal candidates and are for the years 1951–1959. We are assuming that all the British candidates classified as "college or university" have completed their undergraduate work. The figures compare favorably with the data presented by Berrington and Finer. The latter found that 55 percent of the 506 back-bench members of the Conservative and Labor parties had enjoyed university educations. See H. B. Berrington and S. E. Finer, "The British House of Commons" in Jean Meynaud (ed.), "The Parliamentary Profession," *International Social Science Journal*, **13** (1961), 602 and 606.

In addition, the data show that in terms of birthplace, the respondents tended to reflect the distribution of the population in the several geographic areas (see Table 3.4). As the tradition that MPs have local roots and ties is very strong, these latter data are not surprising. Insofar as understanding recruitment patterns is concerned, however, the question arises as to why these legislators were so representative of the ethnic and religious composition of Canadian society, but so remarkably unrepresentative of

TABLE 3.2 MEAN SES SCORES OF PARTY CANDIDATES BY REGION[a] FOR THE PERIOD 1945–1962

| Party | Quebec | Ontario | Residual |
|---|---|---|---|
| Social Credit | $\bar{X}$ SES<br>49.9<br>($N$ = 126) | $\bar{X}$ SES<br>53.0<br>($N$ = 97) | $\bar{X}$ SES<br>50.4<br>($N$ = 200) |
| Conservative | $\bar{X}$ SES<br>71.8<br>($N$ = 273) | $\bar{X}$ SES<br>63.9<br>($N$ = 290) | $\bar{X}$ SES<br>58.8<br>($N$ = 344) |
| Liberal | $\bar{X}$ SES<br>77.2<br>($N$ = 302) | $\bar{X}$ SES<br>67.5<br>($N$ = 291) | $\bar{X}$ SES<br>59.0<br>($N$ = 359) |
| New Democratic | $\bar{X}$ SES<br>56.1<br>($N$ = 90) | $\bar{X}$ SES<br>50.3<br>($N$ = 256) | $\bar{X}$ SES<br>46.9<br>($N$ = 305) |

[a] Residual region includes all of Canada with the exception of the provinces of Quebec and Ontario. The 1961 census data indicated that 81.2 percent of Canada's 5,123,151 French Canadians lived in Quebec. A further 6.8 percent, by far the largest single group, resided in Ontario, and the remaining 17 percent were distributed among eight provinces, the Yukon, and the Northwest Territories.

TABLE 3.3 ETHNIC AND RELIGIOUS ORIGINS OF THE HOUSE OF COMMONS AND NATIONAL POPULATION (percentage)

| | Legislators | National Population |
|---|---|---|
| Ethnic[a] | | |
| British Isles | 51 | 43.8 |
| France | 34 | 30.4 |
| Central Europe (Poland and Germany) | 6 | 7.6 |
| Scandinavia | 6 | 4.5 |
| Eastern Europe (Russia and Ukraine) | 3 | 3.3 |
| Italy | 1 | 2.5 |
| Other | 0 | 7.9 |
| Religious[b] | | |
| Protestant | 49 | 45.8 |
| Catholic | 45 | 45.7 |
| Jewish | 2 | 1.4 |
| Other | 4 | 7.1 |
| | ($N$ = 165) | ($N$ = 18,238,247) |

[a] Other ethnic groups include Asiatics, Indians, Eskimos, Greeks, Turks, and so forth. Scandinavian countries include Iceland as well as Holland, Norway, Sweden, and Denmark.

[b] Other religious groups include Buddhists, Jehovah's Witnesses, and so forth.

TABLE 3.4 BIRTHPLACE OF MPs AND NATIONAL POPULATION (percentage)

| *Birthplace* | *Legislators* | *National Population*[a] |
|---|---|---|
| Maritime Provinces | 13 | 10.5 |
| Quebec | 29 | 28.8 |
| Ontario | 30 | 34.2 |
| Western Canada | 21 | 26.5 |
| Foreign born | 7 | 16.0 |
| | (*N* = 165) | (*N* = 18,238,247) |

[a] This column totals more than 100 percent because the foreign born are also distributed among the other categories.

that society in terms of educational attainment, primary occupation and, to a lesser extent, social background.

An obvious answer is that the high cost of entering and staying in public life in Canada serves as a filter through which thousands of would-be legislators are unable to pass. Until 1963, when their salaries were increased substantially, Canadian MPs were paid only $10,000 per year. Because the parties normally underwrite only a portion of campaign costs, and because virtually every MP finds it necessary to maintain a home both in Ottawa and in his constituency, an aspirant for office generally requires substantial financial resources. Such resources are more likely to be possessed by individuals who are in the business world or who are members of the professions, rather than by people who work at what we have termed low-status occupations. Further, as there is a strong relationship between being in a business or professional category and possessing a superior education, we find a disproportionate number of individuals who have at least an undergraduate degree.

A second reason why these legislators constituted a socioeconomic and educational elite group may be inferred from data gathered in national studies of the American electorate.[13] Such studies indicate that voting turn-out, the frequency with which one discusses politics, and one's interest and involvement in the political process vary strongly with education, occupation, and social class; the higher the social origins, education, and occupation, the greater the tendency to become politically involved. Data we have tend to support these findings. Fully 66 percent of the legislators in the sample said they were raised in homes in which there was considerable political discussion or where family members were active politically; 42 percent of the respondents recalled becoming interested in the political process while they were children; 41 percent said that when they were growing up they belonged to groups or organizations in which politics were discussed; 46 percent had held some elected public office prior to their election to Parliament; 73 percent had held an office in their political parties; and only 18 percent were complete amateurs in that they had never held either public or party office prior to becoming MPs. Again, attesting to the relationship between political interest and activity on one hand, and education and occupation on the other is the fact that 85 percent of the respondents who were in the business-professional category had held some party office as compared with only 66 percent of the legislators whose primary occupations before becoming an MP were of the low status variety. Although Canadian legislators appear to have less political experience than American Congressmen, in comparison with their electors, their interest and political activity were probably extraordinary. Thus, one reason why there are relatively few individuals with rudimentary educations and low occupations is that such people are least likely to have the kind of experiences that would motivate them to become MPs.

The proportion of Catholics we found in our sample might be attributed to the fact that a majority of Canada's Catholics reside in the province of Quebec. Thus they are able to make their votes more effective (in terms of the number of Catholic legislators they elect) than would be the case if, as in the United States, they were fairly evenly distributed geographically. However, the data show that although 50 percent of the Canadian Catholic legislators *were* elected by 55.6 percent of the Catholics residing in Quebec, the remaining 42 percent were elected by the 44.4 percent of Canadian Catholics living outside of Quebec. Furthermore, French Canadians were equally well represented. For example, 77 percent of the French-Canadian legislators in the 25th Parliament represented Quebec, the province which in 1961 had 76.6 percent of all French Canadians residing within its boundaries. The remaining 23.4 percent of the French Canadians who resided outside of Quebec elected the other 23 percent of the French-Canadian legislators.

In no small part, this phenomenon can be attributed to the fact that outside of Quebec the Catholics and French Canadians have never had ascribed to them the kind of inferior status that limits access to high public office. Catholics have been on an equal plane with Protestants[14] since the Quebec Act of 1774, and politicians have neither been advantaged nor disadvantaged by their ethnic or religious backgrounds; it is true that French Canadians have enjoyed their greatest success, nationally, in the Liberal party. In the United States, on the other hand, Catholicism and Judaism, to some extent, are still associated with more recently arrived immigrant groups; they do not have as high a status ascribed to them as do the more conventional Protestant denominations. In fact, Catholic and Jewish aspirants for high public office generally have been disadvantaged in constituences with small proportions of members of their religions.[15]

## POLITICAL SOCIALIZATION

Social psychologists and sociologists frequently employ the concept of socialization to explain how the individual is acculturated, particularly emphasizing how this is accomplished among the very young.[16] The concept, as it is used by political scientists, however, entails something far broader than merely becoming aware of significant others in one's environment. In political science research, political socialization usually is viewed as the process by which an individual acquires political values, attitudes, interest in and knowledge of the political community, the regime, and its institutions and incumbent leaders. In focusing upon the activation of interest we realize, even though interest implies awareness, that we are studying only one component of a very complex process. The data were derived from answers to the question, "How did you first become interested in politics?"[17] The use of a recall question to delineate an event which, in some instances, occurred a half century earlier is a hazardous undertaking. Thus, despite the fact that the findings presented or referred to generally support those of others who have studied political socialization, they should be viewed with caution.

Since Plato, political philosophers have understood that the stability and even the continued viability of a polity are functions of effective political socialization. Despite this there have been relatively few attempts to study the process systematically and quantitatively. As recently as 1959, Heinz Eulau[18] complained, "we know next to nothing about political socialization." Even at the time, however, he was reporting his findings regarding the patterns of political socialization of members of American state legislatures. H. H. Remmers[19] had already studied political attitudes among a national sample of high school students. Since that time, aspects of political socialization have been the subject of fairly intensive research.[20] The assumption that variations in the process of socialization may be a function of intersocietal differences[21] helped to inspire a series of comparative studies of the socialization of children,[22] high school students,[23] adults,[24] and national legislative leaders.[25]

Many propositions concerning detailed aspects and characteristics of the socialization process may be generated from the available research findings. The potential contradictoriness of some is suggested by a brief listing: (1) Socialization begins early, proceeds rapidly but unevenly, and produces a fairly stable product by age sixteen.[26] (2) In socialization, elementary school children acquire both a party identification and a highly valued norm to vote for the best candidate regardless of party.[27] (3) Political socialization and resocialization is continuous, preferences and attitudes being under constant potential change through the influence of friendship and occupational groups.[28] (4) There are numerous agents of socialization that vary with different periods of life.[29] (5) The relative importance of various socializing agents varies, in part, with societal differences.[30] (6) Aspects of the political socialization process vary with intelligence,[31] sex,[32] age,[33] socioeconomic status and background,[34] region,[35] and party affiliation.[36] (7) Variations in the socialization process affect subsequent political behavior, orientations, and attitudes.[37]

To summarize, socialization has been viewed as a childhood or continuous process. It has been seen as a process predominantly influenced by such varied agents as family, schools, and the several peer groups. It has been ascribed the role of producing both particularistic loyalties and universalistic principles. When the evidence consists of discreet partially discordant findings, it is likely that the apparent contradictions could be resolved by specifying the conditions under which a particular proposition holds.[38] For the present, however, we will have to confine ourselves to simply listing our findings for the respondents. In part, these support our previously reported research on the socialization patterns of parliamentary party leaders.[39]

Thus, there was a very strong relationship (Gamma 0.98) between the times and the agents of socialization. Those MPs who recalled being socialized early in life cited primary groups (usually the family) as the socializing agents. If socialization was delayed until adolescence, the socializing agent was one's self. Those legislators who reported that the process did not occur until the adult (postadolescent) stage of the life cycle, cited various external events and conditions in their environments as agents. Consequently, it was again possible to array the respondents along a bidimensional time–agent continuum of socialization, ranging from early-family through adolescence-self to adult-external. Also, a substantial proportion of this elite group of political actors could not recall becoming interested in politics until they were adults. Like their leaders, these MPs tended to cite the depression and other events relating to the war as socializing agents. Similarly, those who socialized early reported that the family was an active agent of socialization. That is, socialization tended to be of a direct rather than indirect nature.[40] As was the case with their leaders, patterns of socialization were only weakly related (Gamma = 0.10) to age differences.

Unlike the findings reported for parliamentary and congressional leaders, however, patterns of political socialization did not vary strongly with differences in socioeconomic backgrounds (Gamma = 0.10) among nonleaders. Also, the socialization process *did* appear to be related to ethnic–religious differences in that there was a correlation of 0.23 between position on a socialization continuum and the possession or lack of French-Catholic cultural characteristics. Finally, the proportion of nonleaders in the early-family position was smaller (39 percent versus 54 percent), and the proportion on the adult-external position of the socialization continuum was larger (45 percent versus 35 percent) than was the case among party leaders.

Perhaps the single most striking aspect of the data was the relationship, also reported by other scholars,[41] between variations in the political socialization process and the level of family political activity. The political activities of the respondents' families were measured by a Political Environment Index. It was constructed from their replies to a number of questions,[42] and has three positions: very political, some politics, and apolitical. The data show that the more active and interested the family was in politics, the greater the tendency toward early socialization by the family (see Table 3.5). Further, when other variables were controlled the relationships between parental political activity and patterns of political socialization remained consistently strong (see Table 3.6).

TABLE 3.5 RELATIONSHIPS BETWEEN POLITICAL SOCIALIZATION AND POSITION ON POLITICAL ENVIRONMENT INDEX[a] (percentage)

| | POSITION ON POLITICAL ENVIRONMENT INDEX | | |
|---|---|---|---|
| *Political Socialization* | *Very Political* | *Some Politics* | *Apolitical* |
| Early–family | 67 | 34 | 21 |
| Adolescence–self | 6 | 26 | 16 |
| Adult–external | 27 | 40 | 63 |
| | ($N$ = 66) | ($N$ = 40) | ($N$ = 51) |
| | | (Gamma = 0.52) | |

[a] The data do not include the eight respondents for whom time and agent of socialization were not correlated.

In summary, the data indicate a relationship between position on the socialization continuum and the possession of French-Canadian cultural characteristics. They also support Eulau, Karlsson, Greenstein, and Almond and Verba's conclusions that one's socialization is a continuous process, and that experiences outside the primary group may influence political attitudes and behavior. However, the strength and durability of the correlations between the level of parental political activity and patterns of socialization also strongly imply that we must be cognizant of and sensitive to the importance of early primary group experiences as determinants of political values, interests, and behavior.[43]

TABLE 3.6 EXAMPLES OF THE STRENGTH OF THE RELATIONSHIP BETWEEN POLITICAL ENVIRONMENT AND SOCIALIZATION WITH OTHER VARIABLES CONTROLLED

| *Relationship between Political Environment and Socialization* | | | |
|---|---|---|---|
| Parliamentary leaders | .75[a] | Nonleaders | .45 |
| Legislators with no French cultural characteristics | .67 | Legislators with all French cultural characteristics | .48 |
| No prior political office experience | .69 | Prior political office experience | .48 |
| 45 years of age and under | .62 | 46 years of age and over | .41 |
| Less than a college education | .56 | College education | .49 |
| Grew up in cosmopolitan environment | .53 | Grew up in a noncosmopolitan environment | .52 |

[a] Particularly intriguing was the strength of the relationship between parental activity and socialization for the parliamentary leaders. Wright, Marvick and Nixon and Valen and Katz reported similarly high levels of political activity among German, American, and Norwegian party leaders.

## POLITICAL RECRUITMENT

The relatively high social origins, early interest in politics, superior educations, and prestigious occupations characteristic of so many Canadian MPs suggest that a substantial proportion generated their own political careers; this is what Samuel J. Eldersveld termed "self-starting." Further, the highly politicized environments in which many were socialized and the fact that strong partisan feelings seem to have been inculcated in them at an early age also suggest that some were initially encouraged by their families to begin a career.[44] However, these characteristics are not in themselves sufficient reasons to explain why they became politically active, as in any society there are thousands of people with similar characteristics who do not become political activists. Thus, Milbraith and Bowman and Boynton[45] suggest that potential activists need to be pushed across some political activity threshold; in many instances, a party organization provides the required push. The data, derived from responses to "Was there any particular person or group who encouraged you to enter politics?" support these theoretical expectations: 23 percent of the MPs indicated that they were self-starters; 13 percent were encouraged to enter active politics by friends, neighbors, and work associates; 11 percent cited their immediate families (parents, siblings); and 53 percent were recruited by the party.[46] Not unnaturally, there were empirical links between political socialization and recruitment patterns. A substantial proportion of the legislators who were socialized early in life either generated their own careers or were encouraged by their families to actively enter politics. There was, therefore, a correlation of 0.24 between early family socialization and self and family recruitment. There also was a correlation of similar magnitude between position on the Political Environment Index and self and family recruitment. The tendency was for legislators raised in families who were active and interested in politics to start their own careers or to claim that their careers were sponsored by their families. Previous research on political recruitment patterns had pointed to a relationship between recruitment practices and the strength of interparty political competition.[47] Heinz Eulau,[48] for example, found a relationship between the competitiveness of a state political system and the frequency with which legislators cited parties as sponsors of their political careers. A similar relationship exists between competition[49] and party recruiting (see Table 3.7). The data suggest that Canadian parties

TABLE 3.7 THE RELATIONSHIP BETWEEN INTERPARTY POLITICAL COMPETITION AND RECRUITMENT BY PARTY (percentage)

| | INTERPARTY POLITICAL COMPETITION | | |
|---|---|---|---|
| *Recruitment* | *Very Competitive* | *Moderately Competitive* | *Not Competitive* |
| Recruited by party | 63 | 47 | 43 |
| Not recruited by party | 37 | 53 | 57 |
| Total | 100 | 100 | 100 |
| | ($N$ = 72) | ($N$ = 47) | ($N$ = 46) |
| | | (Gamma = 0.27) | |

tend to be most active as proselytizers in politically marginal constituencies, and least active in districts that are not politically competitive. As only winning candidates for office are being examined, we can infer that the parties are least active in districts in which they are overwhelmingly favored and most active in constituencies in which the outcome of an electoral contest is in doubt. The relationship between recruitment by party and the level of interparty competition will be explored further in the next section when another aspect of legislative recruitment (circumstances surrounding the candidacies of the subjects) is examined. It should be noted that there was also a relationship (Gamma = 0.30) between the incidence of party recruiting and the age of legislators. Thus, the younger the respondents were (45 and under), the greater was the tendency to be recruited by a party. This is attributed to the growth of party organization and activity concomitant with the increase in Canadian population, industrialization, and urbanization of the last twenty years.

## PREPARLIAMENTARY POLITICAL EXPERIENCE

The two most striking features of the data on preparliamentary political careers are: (1) the amount of political experience the New Democrats had prior to their election to the Commons, and (2) the large proportion of MPs, regardless of party, who had been party activists.

Unlike the members of the other three parties, not one of the New Democrats was a political novice before his election. Further, almost two-thirds of them had held both an elected public office and a position in their own party organization[50] (see Table 3.8).

TABLE 3.8 PREPARLIAMENTARY EXPERIENCE BY PARTY (percentage)

| *Preparliamentary Experience* | *Social Credit* | *Conservative* | *Liberal* | *New Democrat* |
|---|---|---|---|---|
| Held both elected and party office | 18 | 40 | 21 | 62 |
| Held party office only | 66 | 75 | 68 | 100 |
| Held elected office only | 35 | 56 | 34 | 62 |
| Never held any office | 17 | 17 | 21 | |

The large proportion of MPs with prior experience as party officials might be explained, in part, by the generally greater importance of party in a country with a parliamentary system of government. That this is far from a complete explanation, however, is suggested by a comparison of these data with those of Austin Ranney. Ranney[51] found that only 26 percent of 1311 Conservative candidates and 17 percent of 1431 Labor candidates for the British House of Commons had held some local or national office in their respective party organizations. Some of the difference may be explained by the respective samples. Ranney was studying only nonincumbents, and it is quite possible that the proportion of party officeholders would have been higher if his sample had been made up of incumbents, as is the present data.

It seems clear, however, that the proportion of party officeholders in the present sample is high, and that this has implications for the operation of the Canadian parliamentary system. One implication that is suggested immediately is that many Canadian MPs, because of their extensive involvement in party activities, are intensely partisan and committed to their party's positions for some time before their election to Parliament. A second implication is that a local or national party office frequently may be used as a springboard to the House of Commons. In the next section data are presented that suggest that under certain conditions party office indeed may serve as a vehicle to national elected office. First there are presented other data that suggest that the majority of Canadian MPs are not unhappy with their status.

## FUTURE EXPECTATIONS

The legislators' responses to the question, "Are there any other public offices you would like to seek sometime in the future?" reveal what appears to be a very high level of satisfaction with their current positions. Fully 75 percent said there were no other public offices in which they were interested; 9 percent were interested in judgeships[52] or appointments to the Senate; 7 percent wanted to return to provincial politics; 6 percent said they would like to be the mayors of the cities in which they resided; and an additional 3 percent said they were interested in other public offices, but they would not reveal what these were.

It seems reasonable to assume that this relatively high level of satisfaction, in part, stems from the visibility and prestige ascribed to the position of MP and, in part, from the fact that most of the respondents probably felt they "had gone about as far as they could go." That is, there are no elected national offices with the status and powers of the President or Senate to which the MP, like his counterpart in the American House of Representatives, can aspire.

Despite the generally high level of satisfaction, there were some interesting differences among various groups of legislators. For example, the more experienced MPs were more content with their current status than the relative newcomers (legislators with less than six years of parliamentary experience). Legislators whose primary occupations have been classified as low status were less satisfied than the business-professional group (62 percent versus 76 percent). Fully 23 percent of the former group said they would like an appointment (with life tenure) to the Senate, an understandable desire for individuals with limited financial resources.

## *SUMMARY*

In certain respects, the members of this Canadian House of Commons were, like other democratic legislative bodies, very much an elite group.

They compared favorably in terms of occupation and educational attainment with a group of American Senators and nonincumbent candidates for the British House of Commons. The majority had at least one university degree, and were either executives of business corporations, proprietors of their own businesses, or members of professions such as medicine and law prior to their election to the House of Commons. Their social origins were considerably more middle class than were a cross section of the population. However, unlike the members of the American Congress, who generally over-represent the Anglo-Scottish-Irish-Protestant sector of American Society, the legislators in this parliament were remarkably representative of the distribution of ethnic and religious characteristics in Canada. In terms of their places of birth, they were also approximately representative of the distribution of the Canadian population in the several geographic regions. This combination of characteristics can be attributed to the facts that: (1) the cost of entering and sustaining a political career limits the access of lower socioeconomic status groups to institutions like the House of Commons; (2) extensive interest and participation in the political process are confined largely to the well educated and relatively prosperous segment of a society; and (3) candidates for the House of Commons never have been particularly advantaged or disadvantaged by their ethnic–religious backgrounds.

The data show a very strong correlation between the time at which these respondents were socialized politically and the agents of the socialization process. Their positions on a political socialization continuum varied strongly with the level of political activity of their families.

As for actual active entry into politics, slightly over half the sample felt that initially their careers had been sponsored by a political party—data which seem to indicate that Canadian political parties, in part, perform the recruiting function generally ascribed to parties by party theorists. Family, friends, and neighbors were also active recruiters. As one would expect from such an elite group, a substantial proportion (23 percent) generated their own political careers. We found the extent of party recruiting to be related both to the legislators' age differences and the degree of political competition in the constituencies they represented.

In terms of their preparliamentary political experience, the New Democrats were by far the most politically sophisticated group of legislators in that they most frequently had held either a party or an elected public office before becoming MPs. An unusually high proportion, regardless of party, had held a local or national party office prior to their election to Parliament. The majority (75 percent) of the legislators, apparently were well satisfied with their status as national legislators, although there were some variations in the level of satisfaction among them; the younger respondents and those who had worked at low status occupations prior to their incumbency most frequently aspired to other public offices.

# Notes

1. Such quantitative study also has helped to delineate the recruitment patterns of bureaucratic elites and has provided data for some genuine comparisons between the bureaucracies of developed and emerging nations. A good American study was done by Lloyd Warner, Paul Van Riper, Norman Martin, and Orvis Collins, *The American Federal Executive* (New Haven, Conn.: Yale University Press, 1963). For a study of the bureaucracy of an emerging nation, see Ralph Braibanti, "The Higher Bureaucracy of Pakistan" in Ralph Braibanti (ed.), *Asian Bureaucratic Systems Emergent from the British Imperial Tradition* (Durham, N.C.: Duke University Press, 1966), pp. 209–353.

2. Max Weber, "Politics as a Vocation" in Hans Gerth and C. Wright Mills (eds.), *From Max Weber: Essays in Sociology* (New York: Oxford University Press, 1946), pp. 77–128.

3. This is still a much lower figure than the 53 percent of American Senators whom Matthews reported having a law degree. See Donald R. Matthews, *United States Senators and Their World* (New York: Vintage Books, 1960) p. 26. See also Leo Hamon, "Members of the French Parliament," in Jean Meynaud (ed.), "The Parliamentary Profession," *International Social Science Journal,* **13** (1961), 550.

4. See Austin Ranney, *Pathways to Parliament* (Madison, Wis.: University of Wisconsin Press, 1965), pp. 107–225. An analysis of the back-bench members of the British House of Commons (1955–1959) by H. B. Berrington and S. E. Finer indicates that 13 percent of the 270 back-bench Conservative MPs were lawyers. The proportion of Labor MPs who were lawyers apparently is smaller and is contained in the general category "Professions" (31 percent). See H. B. Berrington and S. E. Finer, "The British House of Commons" in Jean Meynaud (ed.), pp. 601 and 605.

5. Alexander Brady, "Canada and the Model of Westminster," in William B. Hamilton (ed.), *The Transfer of Institutions* (Durham, N.C.: Duke University Press, 1964). Although the congruence between politics and law has been cited a number of times to explain the proliferation of lawyers as legislators, the only systematic studies of this empirical phenomenon are those by Joseph Schlesinger, "Lawyers and American Politics: A Clarified View," *Midwest Journal of Political Science* **1** (1957), 26–39; David Derge, "The Lawyer in the Indiana General Assembly," *Midwest Journal of Political Science,* **6** (1962) 19–53; and Heinz Eulau and John Sprague, *Lawyers in Politics: A Study of Professional Convergence* (Indianapolis, Ind.: The Bobbs-Merrill Company, Inc., 1964).

6. Brady, p. 74.

7. The source is the *1961 Census of Canada: Labor Force* (Ottawa: Dominion Bureau of Statistics 1961).

8. Only 5.6 percent of the Canadian population had a university or college education in 1961; fully 85.7 percent had not completed high school. The source is *1961 Census of Canada: Education* (Ottawa: Dominion Bureau of Statistics, 1961).

9. For a multivariate analysis in which this scoring system is employed see Allan Kornberg, *Parties as Recruiters in the Canadian Parliamentary System,* a paper delivered in 1966 at the annual meeting of the American Political Science Association held in New York.

10. The rationale and method for computing the scores are described in Albert J. Reiss *et al., Occupation and Social Change* (New York: The Free Press, 1961).

11. For example, 34 percent of the fathers of Canadian MPs had low status occupations as compared to only 7 percent of the Senate sample studied by Matthews, p. 29.

12. Of the 180 Senators, 75 percent were of northwest European origin (British Isles and Scandinavia) and 88 percent were Protestant. For a more complete comparison see Allan Kornberg and Norman Thomas, "Representative Democracy and Political Elites in Canada and the United States," *Parliamentary Affairs,* **19** (1965–1966), 91–102.

13. See Angus Campbell, Philip E. Converse, Warren E. Miller, and Donald E. Stokes, *The American Voter* (New York: John Wiley & Sons, Inc., 1960), pp. 333–380; Bernard Berelson, Paul Lazarsfeld, and William McPhee, *Voting* (Chicago, Ill.: University of Chicago Press, 1954); and Paul Lazarsfeld, Bernard Berelson, and Hazel Gaudet, *The People's Choice* (New York: Duell, Sloan and Pierce-Meredith Press, 1944). For works that have made use of many of these empirical findings see Seymour M. Lipset, *Political Man* (New York: Doubleday Anchor Books, 1963), and Robert E. Lane, *Political Life* (New York: The Free Press, 1959).

14. This is not to suggest, however, that the French Canadians have *never* experienced either economic or social discrimination. In fact, the so-called "quiet Revolution" in Quebec has attempted, among other things, to make drastic changes in the educational system that generated a substantial proportion of this economic discrimination.

15. Apparently, a Catholic or Jewish political affiliation is a handicap for would-be members of the British House of Commons, particularly if they are Conservatives. Ranney reports that the Conservative Central Office freely admits that anti-semitism is sometimes so strong in local associations that it makes impossible the adoption of a Jew, however well qualified he is on other grounds. On the other hand, religious prejudice is less common among Constituency Labor parties. The Nuffield general election studies show that Labor in 1959 had substantially more Jewish candidates than did the Conservatives (forty-one versus nine), and also more nonconformists (forty-eight versus eight), but fewer Roman Catholics (twenty versus twenty-five). See Ranney, p. 211.

16. For a review of this literature see Irvin L. Child, "Socialization," in Gardner Lindzey (ed.), *Handbook of Social Psychology, II* (Reading, Mass: Addison-Wesley Publishing Company, 1954), pp. 655–692.

17. This is a contraction of two questions used by Heinz Eulau in a study of American State legislators. Eulau's subjects were asked, "How did you become interested in politics?" and "What is your earliest recollection of being interested in it?" See Eulau, *The Legislative System,* p. 79.

18. Heinz Eulau *et al.,* "The Political Socialization of American State Legislators," *Midwest Journal of Political Science,* **3** (1959), 188.

19. For reports of this research see H. H. Remmers, "Early Socialization of Attitudes," in Eugene Burdick and Arthur Brodbeck (eds.), *American Voting Behavior* (New York: The Free Press, 1959), pp. 55–67. See also H. H. Remmers and D. H. Radler, *The American Teenager* (Indianapolis, Ind.: The Bobbs-Merrill Company, Inc., 1957).

20. See Robert D. Hess and Judith V. Torney, unpublished manuscript. Any subsequent references are to this work. The second part of this study is being prepared by David Easton and Jack Dennis but was not available at the time that this manuscript was in preparation. For earlier reports on some of their findings see R. D. Hess and D. Easton. "The Child's Changing Image of the President," *Public Opinion Quarterly,* **24** (1960), 632–644; "Youth and the Political System"

in Seymour M. Lipset and Leo Lowenthal (eds.), *Culture and Social Character: The Work of David Riesman Reviewed* (New York: The Free Press, 1961), pp. 226–251. See also Fred I. Greenstein's important work, *Children and Politics* (New Haven, Conn.: Yale University Press, 1965). All subsequent references are to this work. For earlier reports on Greenstein's research see Fred I. Greenstein, "The Benevolent Leader: Children's Images of Political Authority," *American Political Science Review,* **54** (1960), 934–943, and "More on Children's Images of the President," *Public Opinion Quarterly,* **25** (1961), 648–654. No reports of the research of W. Kent Jenning on the political socialization of American high school students were available when this manuscript was in preparation.

21. See Lucian W. Pye, "Political Modernization and Research on the Process of Political Socialization," *Items,* **13** (1959), 25–28.

22. Robert D. Hess, "The Socialization of Attitudes toward Political Authority: Some Cross-National Comparisons," *International Social Science Journal,* **25** (1963), 542–559.

23. Frank Pinner, "Parental Overprotection and Political Distrust," *The Annals of the American Academy of Political and Social Science* (September 1965), 58–70.

24. Gabriel A. Almond and Sidney Verba, *The Civic Culture* (Princeton, N.J.: Princeton University Press, 1963).

25. Allan Kornberg and Norman Thomas, "The Political Socialization of National Legislative Elites in the United States and Canada," *The Journal of Politics,* **27** (1965), 761–775.

26. Greenstein, *Children and Politics,* p. 73, and Hess and Torney, pp. 371–385. Also, the bulk of the literature on political socialization that Herbert Hyman reviewed suggested that the average American has acquired most of his political values by age sixteen. Herbert Hyman, *Political Socialization* (New York: The Free Press, 1959), pp. 51–68.

27. Hess and Torney feel that the tendency of many American children to see themselves as independent of party affiliation, and the value they ascribe to voting for the best qualified candidates are functions of socialization by the school. Greenstein also noted that the tendency to describe themselves as independents increased with age among New Haven children.

28. See Georg Karlsson, "Political Attitudes among Male Swedish Youth," *Acta Sociologica,* **3** (1958), 236, and Hess and Torney, p. 380. Heinz Eulau also concluded from a study of American state legislators that the time of political socialization was not confined to the preadult period of the life cycle, but, rather, that it could occur at almost any phase of a person's development.

29. Kornberg and Thomas found that among the group of Canadian parliamentary and American congressional leaders they studied: (1) those who recalled being socialized early cited primary groups as the socializing agents, (2) those who socialized during adolescence cited themselves, and (3) those who did not recall being socialized until the postadolescent stage cited various environmental events and conditions. See Kornberg and Thomas, pp. 761–775. On the other hand, Hess and Torney, pp. 376–377, claim that the most important agent of early political socialization is the school rather than the primary group, and that although the family rather early transmits a preference for a political party, its role in most other areas is to reinforce other institutions in teaching political information and orientations to the child.

30. The responses of Canadian parliamentary leaders revealed a conscious attempt on the part of the family to indoctrinate partisan affiliations and attitudes. This was not the case for American congressional leaders. They tended to cite

a law school as the socializing agent much more than did the Canadians. Kornberg and Thomas, pp. 767–768. William E. Wright was impressed by the frequency with which German party leaders in West Berlin cited cataclysmic events, such as the economic depression during the Weimar Republic. See William E. Wright, Political Subcultures and the Socialization of German Party Leaders, unpublished manuscript. Any subsequent references are to this manuscript. For a complete delineation of his findings see "Local Leadership in Two West Berlin Political Parties: SPD and CDU" (Doctoral dissertation, Vanderbilt University, 1966). On the other hand, Philip Abrams and Alan Little found that, although a handful of British political activists were "traumatized into political activity by Suez," the family appeared to be the most important socializing agent for young activists in all three British parties. See Philip Abrams and Alan Little, "The Young Activist in British Politics," *British Journal of Sociology,* **26** (1965), 315–332.

31. Hess and Torney, p. 382.

32. Many of the findings of studies reporting specifically political sex differences, as well as sex differences in behavior (relevant to politics) are summarized by Hyman, Greenstein, and Hess and Torney.

33. Kornberg and Thomas, p. 773.

34. Hess and Torney, p. 383, and Greenstein, p. 94. Kornberg and Thomas, p. 771, also noted that patterns of political socialization among both Canadian and American legislative leaders varied with their socioeconomic backgrounds.

35. Although Greenstein's data show that the mayor was a salient figure in the political world of New Haven school children, he was rarely mentioned by the Chicago children who were the subjects of the study done by Hess and Torney.

36. Wright points out that SPD leaders tend to cite primary groups as socializing agents, while CDU leaders recalled being sensitized to politics by traumatic events.

37. Research carried out in the Minneapolis area by Herbert McClosky and Harold Dahlgren indicates that among adults the strength of identification and loyalty toward a political party is a function of primary group socialization. See Herbert McClosky and Harold Dahlgren, "Primary Group Influence on Party Loyalty, *American Political Science Review,* **58** (1959), 757–776. Marvick and Nixon found a relationship between position held in the party hierarchy and variations in the level of family political activity. Dwaine Marvick and Charles Nixon, "Recruitment Contrasts in Rival Campaign Groups," Dwaine Marvick (ed.), *Political Decision-Makers* (New York: The Free Press, 1961), pp. 193–217. It was also found that the occupancy of a leadership position in a Canadian Parliament was related to variations in the level of family political interest and activity. See Allan Kornberg, "The Social Bases of Leadership in a Canadian House of Commons," *Australian Journal of Politics and History,* **11** (1965), 324–334. Although the data are not always comparative, the high level of family political interest and activity reported by the Norwegian party leaders studied by Henry Valen and Daniel Katz, *Political Parties in Norway: A Community Study* (Oslo: Universitsforlaget, 1964), pp. 278–280, and the parental political activity of German party leaders in West Berlin, suggest that such activity was again related to occupancy of a leadership position. Abrams and Little, p. 330, also were struck by the level of family political activity reported by young British party activists in their sample. They state that "four out of five young activists come from families with a record of political activity; seven in every ten support the same party as their most politically active parent."

38. We are presently engaged in a cross-cultural study of political socialization patterns among party activists in metropolitan areas.

39. Kornberg and Thomas, pp. 761–775.

40. By "direct" is meant the conscious attempt on the part of individuals and groups to inculcate in others political information, values, or expectations. Examples include the efforts of families to develop partisan attachments in children, the civic education programs carried on in schools and by "good government" groups, and the political education activities of unions and business groups. Indirect socialization occurs more subtly and informally. Politically relevant information, values, and expectations are acquired through exposure to the multitude of social and cultural mechanisms by which people are integrated into a society, rather than through conscious and rationally devised processes of indoctrination. Gabriel Almond uses the terms "latent" and "manifest" political socialization. See Gabriel Almond and James Coleman (eds.), *The Politics of Developing Areas* (Princeton, N.J.: Princeton University Press, 1962), pp. 26–33.

41. See Chapter 3, footnote 37.

42. The MPs were asked: (1) Would you say your father was (a) very active in politics, (b) quite active, (c) not active? (2) When you were growing up were there discussions about politics in your home? (yes or no). If yes, would you say there was (a) a great deal of discussion, (b) some discussion? (3) Has any member of your family ever held an elected public office? (4) Has any member of your family ever held a party office? Legislators who answered affirmatively to questions 3 and 4 or who said that their father was very active in politics and that there was a great deal of political discussion in their homes were (for each response) assigned a numerical value of "2." For each negative response they were coded "0." If the information was not ascertained, the interviewee was coded "1" on the assumption that it was equally probable that he would have answered either yes or no. Respondents who answered for questions 1 and 2 that their fathers were quite active in politics and that there was some discussion of politics in their homes also were assigned the intermediary value of "1." Correlations (Gamma), computed among the items ranged in strength from 0.73 to 0.41. No special weighting system was employed, and a respondent's position on the index was arrived at simply by summing his coded responses and arbitrarily establishing cutting points in the scores.

43. This view is supported by Arthur S. Goldberg, "Discerning a Causal Pattern among Data on Voting Behavior," *American Political Science Review,* **60** (1966), 913–922. According to Goldberg, the use of a Simon and Blalock causal model to explain the direction and relatedness of variables such as party identification and partisan attitudes, supports "the positions of . . . those who have urged the importance of the early socialization of political symbols," p. 917.

44. Samuel J. Eldersveld found that a considerable proportion of the party activists in the Detroit area were "self-starters" in that they generated their own political careers. "One third of all present leaders indicated strongly that they made the decision themselves to enter party work. In addition to self-starters and the party, other agents of recruitment were friends and relatives *not* in politics, occupational, ethnic, and other formal nonpolitical groups, as well as 'accidental' involvement." Samuel J. Eldersveld, *Political Parties: A Behavioral Analysis* (Chicago, Ill.: Rand McNally & Company, 1964), p. 128. W. E. Wright (unpublished manuscript), in addition to party and personal predispositions, cites primary groups, peer group activity, and traumatic events as recruitment sources for German party leaders. In their study of party activists in North Carolina and Massachusetts, Lewis Bowman and G. R. Boynton found that approximately 13 percent of their respondents initially become involved in politics because they were asked by friends or relatives. See Lewis Bowman and G. R. Boynton, "Recruit-

ment Patterns among Local Party Officials," *American Political Science Review,* **60** (1966), 667–676.

45. Lester Milbraith, *Political Participation* (Chicago, Ill.: Rand McNally & Company, 1965), pp. 20–21 and Bowman and Boynton, p. 670.

46. It should be noted that a considerable number of those whom we have designated "party-recruited" said that the party officials who sponsored them were also friends or family members. However, in such instances friendships and family were directly linked with party, whereas the others who cited family or friends did not articulate any linkages between such agents and a political party. Hence, we coded the latter as other than party-recruited.

47. The seminal work in this area was carried out by the late V. O. Key. See V. O. Key, *Southern Politics in State and Nation* (New York: Alfred A. Knopf, Inc., 1949), pp. 386–442, and *American State Politics* (New York: Alfred A. Knopf, Inc., 1956), pp. 133–196.

48. Eulau, *The Legilative System,* p. 98.

49. In this study we employ both a measure of competition based upon voting statistics and one based upon the respondents' perceptions of the competitiveness of their districts. The first measure was based on electoral data from the elections of 1953, 1957, 1958, and 1962. Each of the sample constituencies was classified as "very competitive," if two or more parties shared the seat during the period; as "moderately competitive," if one party won three of the four elections for the seat, but in two of the contests, the differences between the winning and runner-up parties was 3 percent or less of the popular vote case; and as "noncompetitive," if one party won three or more elections and in none was the difference between the first two parties less than 3 percent of the popular vote. In this instance, we have employed the objective measure of competition, because it is the party's rather than the legislators' assessment of the situation that is important·

50. The finding that an unusually high proportion of New Democrats were former public office-holders is consonant with figures reported by Henry Valen in his analysis of candidate recruitment in Norway. For example, he showed that 81 percent of the Labor candidates in 1957 had local government experience as compared with 67 percent of the Conservative and 61 percent of the Liberal party candidates. See Valen, "The Recruitment of Parliamentary Nominees in Norway," *Scandinavian Political Studies,* 1 (1966), 153. In an earlier study, W. J. M. Mckenzie found that 47 percent of the 1951 Labor party nominees had experience in local government, whereas the corresponding figure for Conservatives was only 28 percent. See W. J. M. McKenzie, "Local Government Experience of Legislators," in J. C. Wahlke and H. Eulau (eds.), *Legislative Behavior* (New York: The Free Press, 1959), pp. 272–280. This tendency of Labor parties to nominate candidates with prior public office experience is confirmed by Ranney's longitudinal analysis (Ranney, 108 and 198) of candidate recruitment for the years 1951–1964. Ranney found that 36 percent of the Conservatives and 47 percent of the Labor nonincumbents had local government experience.

51. Ranney, pp. 108 and 198.

52. In Canada, all judges and legal officers are appointed rather than elected.

# 4

# Candidacies, Motives, and Legislative Goals

Local party organizations in Canada, as in other Western democracies,[1] in no small way determine the composition of legislative bodies because of the virtual monopoly they have over the making of nominations.[2] Although candidates are sometimes "preselected" by national party leaders, normally,[3] nominations for the office of MP are made by constituency nominating conventions. Unlike the United States, where such business is governed almost entirely by state electoral laws, the structure of and the procedures followed by nominating conventions are largely idiosyncratic—they depend in great part upon the preferences of the local party. Enough data have been presented to strongly suggest that party organizations do not recruit talent from a population pool in which the several social classes are approximately represented. It seems equally probable that organizations do not always get what they want, or, from a functional viewpoint, what legislatures need. Within any political system, economic and other constraints operate to effectively limit choice. Systematic study of the process by which party organizations screen and groom candidates are rare in political science literature.[4] Consequently, in this chapter the circumstances surrounding the candidacies of the respondents are described, and, there is a particular emphasis on motives for becoming a candidate and for sustaining a parliamentary career. In addition, their goals as legislators are catalogued and correlated with their motives. As was the case in Harold Lasswell's[5] classic study of motives underlying recruitment into the politics of forty years ago, private motives still can be displaced to public objects and endowed with public purposes.

## CANDIDACIES

There were two dimensions underlying the responses of a majority of the interviewees to the question, "How did you become a candidate for MP?" The two dimensions were competition and position. Thus, 37 percent said they had obtained the nomination of their parties only after they had defeated one or more aspirants in an intraparty contest. The remaining 63 percent, as they said nothing about having to win their nominations, apparently became the candidates of their parties without a fight.[6]

In terms of position, 60 percent said that their activity and their prominence, or both, in a local party organization helped secure a nomination; 12 percent said they owed the nomination to their visibility as public officeholders; and 11 percent stated that their nomination stemmed both from prominence in the party and previous success in winning public office. The remaining 17 percent said nothing about a political career because their first political activity occurred when they became candidates. Of this 17 percent, thirteen candidates had not even become interested in politics until they were adults; eight started at the top, in that they simply sought a nomination without trying to win election to a lesser public office; one was encouraged by his family to try for a nomination; and all 27 *never* had been active members of any political party until they became candidates for Parliament. Perhaps the most interesting of this group were the eighteen "notables" who apparently were recruited by top party officials because the officials were convinced that they would add lustre to the party's parliamentary delegation or that they could win marginal districts[7] for the party. One, a famous professional athlete, described the circumstances surrounding his candidacy: "I was approached by ______ (national party chairman at the time), a good friend, first, and asked if I would run. Then, Mr. ______, the president of the ______ association, asked me to be their candidate." A cross tabulation of position with intraparty competition indicated that the local party activists most frequently had to fight for the nominations of their party (see Table 4.1).

TABLE 4.1 CIRCUMSTANCES SURROUNDING CANDIDACY OF MPs (percentage)

| *Incidence of Contested Nomination* | *Held no Previous Offices* | *Elected by Local Party* | *Elected by Public*[a] | *Elected by Party and Public* |
|---|---|---|---|---|
| Contested nomination | 25 | 45 | 16 | 33 |
| Uncontested nomination | 75 | 55 | 84 | 67 |
| | ($N$ = 28) | ($N$ = 100) | ($N$ = 19) | ($N$ = 18) |
| | $X^2$ = 8.25 | D.F. = 3.0 | | P < .050 |

[a] These offices ranged from seats on rural school boards to membership (in some cases, in the Cabinets) in the several provincial legislatures.

Apparently, there were three ways in which a local party position could be used to obtain a nomination.[8] First, one could be "personally chosen" (in the words of a number of respondents) by the former MP in the event of the latter's retirement or defeat, *if* one had been president or chairman of the constituency organization and had worked to elect or re-elect the former MP. Such nominations were rarely contested. A second route to candidacy was to work one's way up in the organization and to establish a wide claim as one deserving of the nomination. Such nominations were also rarely contested. A third springboard to the nomination was to use the position of local party leader to promote one's own candidacy or to have it promoted by one's friends. Such respondents frequently said that they agreed to stand for the nomination only after they had made a long and (seemingly) fruitless search for a suitable candidate. Although they agreed to become a candidate only after considerable persuasion, their candidacies were the ones most likely to be contested. The following response is typical: "I was chairman of the ______ association in my riding. My duty was to find a candidate. All the time, the other leaders of the association felt I would be the most suitable candidate. They kept pressuring me to accept a nomination and finally I gave in and agreed and won it over two others."

These findings offer empirical support for the claim made by Dawson and Ward concerning the crucial role played by local party organizations in the recruitment process, and also provide an interesting supplement to Austin Ranney's data. In his exhaustive study of the recruitment of candidates for the British House of Commons, Ranney[9] found that local organizations played a very important role in the selection process. (This is contrary to the popular notion that in Britain local party associations merely select a candidate from a national party list made available by party headquarters.)

"Most (Conservative) selection committees are dominated by a few members who take their lead from the chairman, he in turn is the key figure in the whole selection process." As well, constituency Labor parties were "every bit as zealous as Conservative associations of their prerogative of adopting candidates."[10]

A substantial proportion of the respondents were expected to use prior public office experience as a vehicle to a nomination for, as Ranney says,[11] "having served on a local council is good evidence that an aspirant has a practical knowledge of government matters, and it also proves that he can win an election." Consequently, it was rather surprising to find that, although 46 percent had held some lesser public office only 12 percent indicated that this experience was *instrumental* in securing a nomination. An additional 11 percent attributed their nomination in part to their visibility and past success as public office-holders.

## MOTIVES FOR CANDIDACY

Heinz Eulau[12] has written that for most state legislators politics is very much a sideline, and the decision to run for a legislative office is not comparable to choosing a nonpolitical occupation or profession. On the other hand, the politician's eternal claim that he is making a sacrifice in embarking upon a public career implies that for him such a decision *is* of major importance. At any rate, individuals considering becoming candidates for the Canadian House of Commons might make such a claim with some justice. As has been indicated, the financial compensation received by Canadian MPs, is small, and the costs of campaigning and maintaining two residences generally are large. The rate of attrition for MPs also is high—approximately 40 percent every election. Since the majority of individuals who become national legislators usually have enjoyed considerable success in business or other professions, the prospect of interrupting a lucrative career for what may be, in many cases, only a very temporary stay probably is not too enticing. In some respects the decision to become a candidate for MP well may be a major one, and we would expect that a certain number of the interviewees would be apprehensive about throwing their hats into the ring.

On the other hand, for some individuals the prospect of becoming a member of a highly prestigious and visible national decision-making body probably would be extremely attractive. Further, as a high level of education, a prestigious occupation, and extensive political activity are related both to a kind of moral imperative to serve the public, and to a feeling that one is competent to do so,[13] one would expect individuals with the backgrounds of these respondents to *want* to become MPs out of a desire to serve the public and to initiate or influence public policy at a national level.

The data fit these expectations rather well. In response to the question, "Why did you become a candidate for MP?" there were 22 percent who said they were extremely reluctant and that they only agreed to become candidates after considerable pressure had been placed upon them. Despite the fact that these claims may not have been entirely valid, these respondents will be referred to as "unmotivated." Another 23 percent claimed that they were motivated either by a desire to initiate or affect legislative policies or to serve their country, constituency, or a particular social group within their constituency. These will be termed "policy–service" motives. Closely related to these expressed motives were those motives (21 percent) couched in distinct ideological terms, such as a desire to safeguard the party system or to achieve a more egalitarian society. The remaining 34 percent, although they rationalized it in different ways, were motivated by an apparent simple and powerful desire to become MPs; these will be referred to as "personal predispositions."[14] The motives differed markedly from those articulated by the Pennsylvania state legislators studied by Frank Sorauf, only in the larger proportion of ideologues and the smaller group of personally predisposed among them (see Table 4.2).

TABLE 4.2 A COMPARISON OF THE MOTIVES EXPRESSED BY CANADIAN MPs AND PENNSYLVANIA STATE LEGISLATORS (percentage)

| *Motives* | *Canadian MPs* | *Pennsylvania Legislators*[a] |
|---|---|---|
| Unmotivated (asked to run) | 22 | 24 |
| Policy–service | 23 | 15 |
| Ideological | 21 | 7 |
| Personal predispositions | 34 | 50[b] |
| | ($N$ = 165) | ($N$ = 106) |

[a] This column total does not equal 100 percent because the data for 4 percent of the respondents were not ascertained.

[b] Under personal predispositions we have grouped what Sorauf classified as, "interest in politics," "dissatisfaction with incumbent," and "miscellaneous, including personal."

Typical examples of the motives cited by Canadian legislators were:

As I told you, I didn't want to become a candidate for MP at the time but was forced into it by some friends in the party and in the legal profession in ________. They insisted that even if I didn't win it would help build my reputation. They were working so hard for me that I felt I just couldn't let them down. I surprised myself and them too by winning.

Because of a sincere desire to affect policy changes that would help the people in ________.

Because I felt that West wasn't getting, and had never gotten, proper treatment. I felt it would under John Diefenbaker, and I wanted to help him.

My background, I suppose. I felt that anyone who had the kind of training and education I had, had a duty to serve.

Because I am working for the principles of the Social Credit party. I felt that our financial principles could only be achieved at the national level where we could control the Bank of Canada.

I felt that in the federal field there was a possibility of doing more for socialism. It gives a man a more important forum to speak from than in the provincial field.

I felt that there was a job to be done in making an election fight out of what looked like a hopeless situation. I believe in the two-party system and in competition. I felt I just had to make a contest out of it.

Because I've always wanted to be an MP, or at least since I got out of the army in 1945.

Well, as I said, I've always been interested in politics, even as a boy. I've always felt I wanted to go into public life—never any doubt. I ran unsuccessfully for member of the Legislative Assembly when I was still a law student.

Just because I wanted to. I just made up my mind to become an MP. I told my family so, even though they were against it.

I admit I sought the nomination actively. I told you I was defeated twice. I love public life. I told everyone I would be an MP by the time I was fifty, and I was.

Although it has been necessary to distinguish, analytically, between an individual's involvement in active politics and his actual recruitment for the position of legislator, there are empirical links between the two events, one of which already has been commented upon. Seventeen percent of the respondents never were active in politics before they became candidates, and thus their initial recruitment and the recruitment for the position of legislator occurred simultaneously. A cross tabulation of patterns of initial recruitment with circumstances surrounding the legislators' candidacies also revealed that (1) the most politically sophisticated candidates (as measured by positions held at the time) were legislators who were initially encouraged by their families to begin political activity, while the least politically sophisticated were those initially recruited by the party and the self-starters; and (2) legislators who were initially recruited by parties had to face intraparty contests for the nomination less frequently than did the others[15] (see Table 4.3).

Insofar as the relationship between first involvement and motives for

TABLE 4.3 PATTERN OF INITIAL RECRUITMENT BY POSITION AND CONTESTED–UNCONTESTED NOMINATION AT TIME OF CANDIDACY (percentage)

| | Pattern of Initial Recruitment | | | |
|---|---|---|---|---|
| | *Self-Starter* | *Family* | *Friends and Neighbors* | *Party Recruited* |
| *Position held* | | | | |
| No position | 24 | 5 | | 21 |
| Party office | 58 | 73 | 64 | 59 |
| Public office | 5 | | 27 | 12 |
| Party and public office | 13 | 22 | 9 | 8 |
| *Frequency of contested candidacies* | | | | |
| Contested | 55 | 56 | 46 | 23 |
| Uncontested | 45 | 44 | 54 | 77 |
| | ($N$ = 38) | ($N$ = 18) | ($N$ = 22) | ($N$ = 87) |

becoming candidates goes, the data indicated that those who initially were recruited by the party tended to claim more frequently (30 percent) than did the others, that they were pressured to become candidates. As one would expect, the original self-starters were the most anxious to become candidates (only 8 percent said they were pressured).

There was an interesting relationship between the distribution of motives and the proportions of contested and uncontested nominations, in that those whose nominations were contested were precisely the ones who most wanted, for a variety of personal reasons, to become MPs (see Table 4.4).

TABLE 4.4 RELATIONSHIP BETWEEN CONTESTED–UNCONTESTED NOMINATIONS AND MOTIVES FOR BECOMING CANDIDATES (percentage)

| *Motives* | *Contested* | *Uncontested* |
|---|---|---|
| Personal predisposition | 54 | 21 |
| Policy–service–ideological | 41 | 48 |
| Not motivated (pressured) | 5 | 31 |
| | ($N$ = 61) | ($N$ = 104) |
| | Gamma = 0.64 | |

## POLITICAL COMPETITION AND CANDIDACIES

As was previously indicated, studies by V. O. Key, Heinz Eulau, and others[16] have demonstrated that there is a relationship between patterns of party recruitment and the party's competitive position. Specifically, it appears that in one-party or predominantly one-party areas the favored party has little difficulty recruiting attractive candidates and workers, while the less-favored organization must work extremely hard to recruit live bodies. Our data indicated a relationship between the political competition in the several sample constituencies and the degree to which party, as opposed to other agents, initially involved people in political activity. The data also shows traces of a relationship between the competitiveness of the constituencies and the positions the legislators held at the time they became candidates. Thus, the largest proportion of very competitive constituencies were represented by individuals who, at the time of their nominations, were local party organization leaders; the most politically experienced (those holding both party and public office) were found in the least competitive districts.

When interparty competition was cross-tabulated with the incidence of contested candidacies, we found that the respondents most frequently had to compete for a nomination in districts in which their party was heavily favored to win (see Table 4.5). When positions held at the time of can-

TABLE 4.5 RELATIONSHIP BETWEEN COMPETITIVENESS OF CONSTITUENCIES AND FREQUENCY OF CONTESTED CANDIDACIES (percentage)

| | INTERPARTY POLITICAL COMPETITION | | |
|---|---|---|---|
| *Candidacies* | *Very Competitive* | *Moderately Competitive* | *Not Competitive* |
| Uncontested | 70 | 64 | 52 |
| Contested | 30 | 36 | 48 |
| | ($N$ = 72) | ($N$ = 47) | ($N$ = 46) |
| | | Gamma = 0.35 | |

didacy were controlled, the direction of the relationship remained the same, although there were differences in the magnitude of the correlation. Thus, regardless of the extent of their political experience when they became candidates, the respondents found it hardest to get an uncontested nomination in districts in which their party was the popular favorite. Of all the interviewees, those who were local party officials at the time found it the most difficult to get a nomination in a noncompetitive district; respondents who had either been elected to public office previously, or who both were party and public officeholders, found it the least difficult to get an uncontested nomination in a noncompetitive district.

In summary, Canadian political parties in the several constituencies seemed to work hardest to involve people initially in political activity in areas that were really competitive. In some cases, initial involvement meant starting at the top (that is, contesting a parliamentary seat). The data suggested that the parties tended to recruit and literally give a nomination to a political novice (in the sense that the recruitee did not have to compete for it) *if* the novice was a prestigious individual or if he could win a doubtful seat for the party. In the eyes of party officials, these attractive novices would give the party enough of an "edge" in competitive districts to win.

In the majority of cases, however, initial recruitment was for a position in the local party organization or as a candidate for local office. In time, it would seem, service in the local organization and, less frequently, experience in a lesser elected office could be used as a springboard to a party's nomination for MP. In the majority of cases (63 percent), either through lack of other candidates or because of behind-the-scene arrangements, the nomination was achieved without an intraparty fight. When such an open struggle did occur, it was most likely to take place in a constituency in which the party's nomination was tantamount to election. The most politically experienced, either through their own efforts or as a result of the decision of other party officials, were most likely to obtain, without a contest, a nomination which practically ensured their election. Local party officials had to fight for their nominations, particularly if they had been given the job of recruiting a suitable candidate and then had decided or allowed themselves to be persuaded that they alone had the necessary qualifications for office.

A substantial proportion of the interviewees, however, were not initially recruited by a political party, but either generated their own careers or were encouraged to begin a political career by families, friends, neighbors, and peer groups. Self-starting and family recruiting occurred most frequently when the individuals were socialized early in families actively involved in politics. The majority (particularly those recruited by the family) tended to be local party officials at the time of their nomination. As they were also considerably more likely than those initially recruited by the party to receive their nominations without a public contest, we may infer that they had established a claim to the nomination because of a fairly long career on behalf of other or former candidates.

Insofar as motives for becoming candidates for Parliament were concerned, it was found that the respondents ranged from those who said they were pressured and unmotivated, through those inspired by a desire to serve the public, to initiate or affect public policy at the national level, and to restructure or maintain certain institutions and procedures in Canadian society, to those who either because of status, the opportunity for power, or other considerations, had a strong desire to be an MP. These motives were not randomly distributed but, instead, varied with the backgrounds of the interviewees. Thus, a smaller proportion of self-starters than others said that they were pressured to become candidates. Those who wanted to become legislators for a variety of personal reasons were most likely to have to fight for their nominations. In the next section we will test theoretical notions concerning the motives of major party candidates and French Canadians as opposed to candidates of other cultural backgrounds. First we will try to determine how, if at all, their motives for becoming candidates were related to motives for sustaining their parliamentary careers.

## MOTIVES FOR SUSTAINING A LEGISLATIVE CAREER

If an individual's initial expectations for a legislative position were completely unaffected by the environment in which he would be placed once he took office, one would expect that his motives for originally becoming a candidate and wanting to stay in the legislature would be perfectly correlated. As our assumption is that initial expectations are supplemented, and at times modified, by values and perspectives developed after incumbency we assumed that there would be some changes in motives from the time they became candidates. For example, we did not expect everyone who cited ideological reasons for becoming a candidate to be an ideologue once he actually had some experience in office, but we did expect a substantial proportion of those initially motivated by policy considerations still to be concerned with policy after becoming incumbents.

The data derived from the question, "If for some reason you had to give up being an MP next week, what would you miss most about the job?" supported our expectations. Fully 31 percent said they would miss the opportunity to initiate or to have an effect upon certain policies in which they were interested, to perform services, or to do things for their constituents. Another 17 percent were moved by ideological considerations, such as the desire to establish a socialist government, or to restore the free enterprise system. The largest proportion (43 percent) were fascinated by the legislative position for a variety of social–psychological reasons. The reasons most frequently cited were: (1) the excitement of being at the center of things and making crucial national decisions, (2) the opportunity to affect Canadian history, and (3) the friendships within the legislature. Only 9 percent of the respondents were not happy with their positions as MPs, and either explicitly or by implication stated that they were not prepared to seek re-election. Thus, although the proportions citing them had changed, the MPs still cited the same kinds of motives for sustaining legislative careers as they had offered for becoming candidates (policy, service, ideological, and personal predispositions).

If we exclude, for the moment, the respondents who claimed that they were pressured into becoming candidates and those who did not want to maintain their careers, we find a correlation of 0.24 between motives for becoming candidates and motives for remaining in office. If the ideologically motivated are combined with the policy–service oriented, the correlation increases to 0.42 (see Table 4.6). As for the initially "reluctant dragons,"

TABLE 4.6 RELATIONSHIP BETWEEN MOTIVES FOR BECOMING A CANDIDATE AND FOR SUSTAINING A LEGISLATIVE CAREER (percentage)

| | WHY BECOME A CANDIDATE | |
|---|---|---|
| *Why Sustain Career* | *Policy–Service–Ideological* | *Personal Predisposition* |
| Policy–service–ideological | 63 | 41 |
| Personal predispositions | 37 | 59 |
| Total | 100 | 100 |
| | ($N$ = 68) | ($N$ = 51) |
| | Gamma = 0.42 | |

11 percent of these were unhappy with their careers, 48 percent expressed motives of policy, service, and ideology, and the remaining 41 percent were now very much attracted by their positions as MPs. The responses of the aforementioned (9 percent) who *were* unhappy about their parliamentary careers reveal a degree of disillusionment and even bitterness which is fascinating. The most extreme statement from these individuals was the following:

> What would I miss? I would miss the countless demands made upon me by people who are under the impression I'm an employment agency. They come for jobs I can't get them and then get mad because I can't. I would miss having to go to affairs with people I have no interest in or having to contribute money, being milked by anyone coming along looking for a handout.

I would miss being talked about by my dear constituents, that I'm drunk or that my marriage is on the rocks.

As Canadian parties must recruit candidates for constituencies in which there is considerable doubt about the outcome of an electoral contest, it can be theorized that in their efforts to maximize their chances of winning they sometimes are forced to "hard sell" attractive but reluctant candidates on the desirability of carrying the party's standard. At times they probably paint a too rosy picture of life in Parliament; when these expectations are not fulfilled, disillusionment and despair result. Those most likely to be disillusioned by the realities of political life are those who have had the least experience in politics—the novices who are sometimes recruited and nominated by a party despite the fact that they never have held either public or party office.

Although the theory is an interesting one, it has a serious weakness—it is unsupported by the data. For, rather than the political innocents being disillusioned with their status,[17] it was the former local party activists who made up the majority (73 percent) of the respondents who did not wish to maintain their parliamentary careers. Ten of these eleven former local party leaders did not have to compete for their party's nomination. All had either been coopted by former MPs or had a widely recognized claim to the nomination resting on their long service in the party organization. The fact that disillusionment with a legislative career was most prevalent *not* among the former amateurs who conceivably might be reacting to the glowing pictures painted by the party pros, but among the former pros themselves is intriguing and is another aspect of legislative behavior that requires further investigation.

## MAJORITY-MINORITY STATUS AND MOTIVES

American political parties frequently are described as "brokerage" organizations that are weak in principle, devoid of ideological commitment, and inclined to differ chiefly over trivia. Coupled with the necessity of building a majority coalition of electors, the brokerage function presumably discourages both parties from postulating distinct, coherent, and enduring ideologies. To promulgate an ideology, it is argued, the parties would risk alienating large groups of voters who do not share their beliefs. The parties, like supermarkets, go where customers are to be found, and one set of leaders is content to play "Tweedledum" to the other's "Tweedledee."[18]

In contrast are the ideological parties of a multiparty system, which presumably appeal to their supporters through sharply defined and tightly constrained sets of ideological beliefs. Such parties are encouraged to maintain their ideological militancy and distinctiveness; to behave otherwise would facilitate the predatory incursion among their supporters of the party or parties closest to them on the ideological continuum.

In the same manner, minor parties in a "two-party plus" system also can afford an ideology and the retention of purity. Since they have no real hope of winning control of the Government, they need not fear irritating those who do not share their policy positions. Further, if they soften or blur their ideological beliefs, they risk weakening the loyalty of the faithful minority upon whom their continued existence depends.

The data, while not intended to test the validity of these assumptions, are, nevertheless, interesting in that they show that a larger proportion of the Social Credit and New Democratic MPs initially were motivated to become candidates for the House by ideological considerations (for example, to establish a socialist or free enterprise system). Although the proportions declined somewhat, more Social Creditors and New Democrats than Conservatives and Liberals cited ideological motives for sustaining their parliamentary careers (see Table 4.7). Particularly intriguing, in light of the

TABLE 4.7 MOTIVES FOR BECOMING A CANDIDATE AND FOR SUSTAINING A PARLIAMENTARY CAREER BY PARTY[a] (percentage)

| | Social Credit | | Conservative | | Liberal | | New Democrat | |
|---|---|---|---|---|---|---|---|---|
| *Motives* | *Why Become a Candidate* | *Why Sustain Career* | *Why Become a Candidate* | *Why Sustain Career* | *Why Become a Candidate* | *Why Sustain Career* | *Why Become a Candidate* | *Why Sustain Career* |
| Not motivated | 8 | 9 | 24 | 8 | 23 | 11 | 22 | 8 |
| Policy and service | 22 | 22 | 29 | 30 | 15 | 30 | 31 | 54 |
| Ideological | 65 | 56 | 10 | 6 | 16 | 16 | 39 | 23 |
| Personal predisposition | 5 | 13 | 37 | 56 | 46 | 43 | 8 | 15 |
| | (*N* = 23) | | (*N* = 66) | | (*N* = 63) | | (*N* = 13) | |

[a] The actual strength of the parliamentary delegations of the four parties were: Social Credit, 30; Progressive Conservative, 116; Liberal, 100; and New Democrat, 19.

aforementioned assumption that minority parties with no serious pretensions to power are those best able to afford an overt ideological commitment, is the fact that the right-wing Social Credit group was so much more ideologically motivated than the left-wing New Democrats. Any analysis of national electoral results will reveal that the probability of the Social

Credit party winning a national election in the foreseeable future is small. Although the probability of the New Democratic party forming a Government or even the Official Opposition in the next decade is not great, the party's future in Canadian politics appears to be relatively glittering in comparison with its adversary on the right of the Canadian political continuum.

## MOTIVES AND FRENCH-CANADIAN CULTURAL CHARACTERISTICS

The data on motives also enable us to test one of the assumptions underlying the aforementioned culturalist theory of Canadian legislative behavior.[19] According to this theory, French Canadians become legislators not for ideological or policy reasons but because of status and other personally instrumental considerations. These personal considerations would be included under what we will term personal predispositions. To test the validity of these assumptions, the respondents' motives for becoming legislators and for staying in Parliament were cross tabulated with their positions on a French-Canadian Cultural Index.[20] It encapsulates those subcultural factors that presumably make French-Canadian political behavior fundamentally different from the behavior of others (see Fig. 2). The data indi-

FIGURE 2. Correlation Matrix showing the interrelation of items on the French-Canadian Cultural Index.

| | *Catholic* | *French Canadian* | *Born in Quebec* | *Parochial Education* | *Educated in Quebec* | *Church Attender* |
|---|---|---|---|---|---|---|
| Catholic | | .98 | .95 | .94 | .96 | .85 |
| French Canadian | | | .96 | .90 | .97 | .76 |
| Born in Quebec | | | | .93 | .99 | .61 |
| Parochial education | | | | | .96 | .75 |
| Educated in Quebec | | | | | | .63 |
| Frequent church attender (at least once a week) | | | | | | |

cate that respondents who possessed all the French characteristics were *least* motivated by personal predispositions and *most* motivated by ideological considerations (see Table 4.8).

If personal predispositions, as compared to other motives, are compared for the three groups of legislators, there are correlations of —0.27 and

TABLE 4.8 Motives for Becoming a Legislator and for Sustaining a Career by Position on the French-Canadian Cultural Index (percentage)

| | *All French Characteristics* | *Some French Characteristics* | *No French Characteristics* |
|---|---|---|---|
| Why Become a Candidate | | | |
| Not motivated | 11 | 24 | 26 |
| Policy–service | 21 | 26 | 19 |
| Ideological | 43 | 18 | 9 |
| Personal predisposition | 25 | 32 | 46 |
| Why Sustain Career | | | |
| Disappointed | 9 | 7 | 12 |
| Policy–service | 23 | 32 | 38 |
| Ideological | 36 | 14 | 7 |
| Personal predisposition | 32 | 47 | 43 |
| | ($N$ = 44) | ($N$ = 79) | ($N$ = 42) |

—0.14 for becoming legislators and staying on in Parliament, respectively. Contrary to the culturalist assumption, it was not the French Canadians who were motivated by personal predisposition. To the extent that there was a relationship between motives and French background (as opposed to other cultural characteristics) it was in the opposite direction.

However, the data also indicate that a majority of the Social Creditors were in the "all French characteristics" category, and that a large proportion of them cited ideological motives rather than personal predispositions for becoming candidates and staying on in Parliament. Thus, it might be argued that the differences in motives (illustrated in Table 4.8) actually were derived from party rather than from culture. When the motives of Social Creditors with all the French cultural characteristics were compared with the motives of Liberal and Conservative respondents with similar backgrounds, it became clear that party affiliation *was* an important explanatory variable (see Table 4.9).

The salience of a Social Credit affiliation (as opposed to another party affiliation) is illustrated if we look at the previous correlations between motives and position on the French-Canadian Cultural Index, first with the French-Canadian Social Creditors included and then with them excluded from the sample (see Table 4.10). When this is done, strong relationships are sharply attenuated and, in one instance, there is actually a change in the direction of the relationship. Even so, these data offer little comfort

TABLE 4.9 MOTIVES FOR BECOMING A LEGISLATOR AND FOR SUSTAINING A LEGISLATIVE CAREER FOR LEGISLATORS WITH FRENCH-CANADIAN CULTURAL CHARACTERISTICS ONLY

| | *French Canadian Social Creditors* | *French-Canadian Liberals and Conservatives* |
|---|---|---|
| Why Become a Candidate | | |
| Not motivated (pressured) | 9 | 13 |
| Policy–service | 19 | 22 |
| Ideological | 67 | 22 |
| Personal predisposition | 5 | 43 |
| | Ideological versus other motives: Gamma = 0.73 | Personal predisposition versus other motives: Gamma = −0.87 |
| Why Sustain Career | | |
| Disappointed | 9 | 9 |
| Policy–service | 24 | 22 |
| Ideological | 52 | 22 |
| Personal predisposition | 15 | 47 |
| | (N = 21) | (*N* = 23) |
| | Ideological versus other motives: Gamma = 0.56 | Personal predisposition versus other motives: Gamma = −0.69 |

TABLE 4.10 CORRELATIONS BETWEEN POSITION ON THE FRENCH-CANADIAN CULTURAL INDEX AND MOTIVES FOR BECOMING CANDIDATES, AND SUSTAINING LEGISLATIVE CAREERS (FOR ALL RESPONDENTS AND WITH SOCIAL CREDITORS REMOVED FROM SAMPLE)

| | *For all Legislators* | *Without Social Creditors* |
|---|---|---|
| Why Become a Candidate X Position on Cultural Index | | |
| Ideological versus other motives | .56 | .28 |
| Personal predisposition versus other motives | −.27 | −.08 |
| Why sustain a Career X Position on Cultural Index | | |
| Ideological versus other motives | .61 | .21 |
| Personal predisposition versus other motives | −.14 | .09 |
| | (*N* = 165) | (*N* = 142) |

to the extreme culturalists for they show that (1) French-Canadian legislators in the Liberal and Conservative parties *still* were somewhat more ideologically inspired, both to become candidates and to stay in Parliament, than were their party colleagues who sprang from other than French-Canadian cultural backgrounds; and (2) they neither were more nor less affected by personal predispositions than the others. (As will be shown in Chapters 5 and 6, the culturalist assumptions concerning the goals and representational role perceptions of French-Canadian legislators also appear to be unsupported by the data.)

## LEGISLATIVE GOALS

The extent to which Canadian MPs share the assumption that the purpose of legislative leaders is to make laws is illustrated dramatically by their replies to the question, "What are the most important things you want to accomplish as an MP?" Responses revealed that 47 percent had goals that in some way were oriented toward the formulation or evaluation of legislative policies. Another 23 percent had goals that were structured either in terms of their constituencies or individual social groups within their constituencies. The remaining 30 percent did not articulate such policy or constituency-oriented goals singularly, but combined these orientations.

As goal selection is a cognitive process that occurs in the mind of the individual legislator, it was not surprising that some legislators were able to perceive their goals very clearly, while others had only vague or fuzzy notions of them; some legislators had very specific and concrete goals while the goals of others were very broad and general. However understandable, it made for a considerable coding and analysis problem. To facilitate the analysis, therefore, the goals expressed by respondents were arrayed along a "goals dimension." At one end of this dimension were placed all those legislators whose goals entailed some desire to initiate or evaluate legislative policies. In the middle were placed those who combined an interest in legislative policy with a more parochial orientation toward their districts. Finally, on the far end of the goals dimension were placed those legislators whose goals were focused upon and structured in terms of their constituencies. These variations in the legislators' purposive role orientations have been termed "policy," "mixed," and "area."

### POLICY-ORIENTED GOALS

The goals of the legislators who were policy-oriented (47 percent) ranged the whole policy continuum. There were, for example, those who expressed goals that were characterized by a quality of remoteness from the day-to-day policy concerns of most legislative leaders. Others were interested in more concrete policies such as finance and trade. A third group had very specific interests in various subfields of legislation. The following are typical responses from legislators whose goals were oriented toward policy:

I want to make some contribution to the maintenance of peace. I'm a World Federalist, not formally really, but I do feel that international understanding can only come when nations, as such, disappear. I'm trying in my own small way to bring this about.

I want to further the program of labor legislation which my party and I as an individual are interested in.

I'm interested in pension rights. Miners and other occupational groups like them move around a lot and lose the pension rights which they've built up when they move. What I am trying to get is national portable pension plan legislation that will correct this.

### MIXED GOALS

The legislators who had mixed goals (30 percent) combined a parochial interest in their constituencies with an interest in policy that ranged from the most general to the most specific. The following comments are typical of the goals this group expressed:

My first objective is to further the principles of liberalism and the Liberal party. Mackenzie King had a great influence on me. He was a great teacher as well as a politician, you know. He impressed on us a way of life, a respect for the traditional liberal ideas of the greatest good for the greatest number, and freedom of the individual. Locally, I've always looked after the civil servants and I'm interested in urban development.

To help the Liberal party and its program for Canada. I feel that we have always been better organized to run this country than any other party. Through the party I can do something to help the low income people of my constituency who need help.

### AREA-ORIENTED GOALS.[21]

As the interests of legislators whose goals were focused solely upon their constituencies (23 percent) were considerably narrower than were those of other legislators, they tended to have goals that were well structured and concrete. Typical of the responses of legislators with area-oriented goals are the following:

I want to help the fruit and vegetable industry in my district. I'm big on airports too!

> I've always had a local outlook. My constituency was neglected by the Liberals. I've concerned myself chiefly with improving fishing. The most important thing a member can do is to look after the people in his riding, regardless of party.

As legislators in democratic political systems are expected to be the advocates as well as the defenders of popular demands, the fact that approximately one-quarter of the interviewees structured their goals in terms of their constituencies, or even in terms of particular social groups therein, is not surprising. Nor is it strange that another 30 percent linked constituency-centered goals with goals oriented toward policymaking. What is surprising is the fact that the largest group structured their goals solely in policy-innovating or policy-evaluating terms. It already has been pointed out that although institutionalized opportunities exist for mass member participation in policy evaluation, the opportunity for the average Canadian MP to actually initiate or to seriously affect the substantive content of a Government's legislative program is rather limited. There are, of course, instances when hard-working and united opposition members can, by an all-out attack, force a Government to make concessions or to withdraw a particular piece of legislation. The change that the opposition parties forced in the Liberal Government budget proposals in 1963 is a case in point. There also is a behind-the-scene opportunity for back bench members of a Government party to substantively influence public policy proposals. The opportunity occurs in the party caucus before the beginning of a session when the various ministers "try out" their proposals on party colleagues. In this testing stage the determined opposition of a substantial group of his party colleagues can result in a minister holding up, altering, or even withdrawing proposed legislation. However, this does not mean that the party leaders necessarily will consider alternative proposals from private members, so that this kind of impact on policy largely is negative.

Essentially the same process is repeated in the opposition party caucuses with the exception that their policy programs largely are intended to attract the sympathetic approval of an attentive national audience rather than to receive the endorsement of Parliament. If we assume that ultimately the Official Opposition will have the opportunity (as the next Government) to put some of their proposals into effect or, if in time, that the governing party will be able to incorporate opposition party policy suggestions into their own program, we can conceive the opposition parties as having an indirect and substantive influence on enacted legislation. Such participation in the policy process obviously is qualitatively and quantitatively different from that of the Canadian MPs counterpart in a legislature such as the American Congress. In the Congress, the individual legislator is much more of a free agent, in that he is not bound by stringent party discipline nor by the feelings that he is obliged to support, on a continuous basis, the policy proposals of his party.[22] Although a considerable proportion of his time is spent in evaluating the policy proposals of the Administration, there is still considerable opportunity for the legislator to initiate policy and to try to translate it into legislation. Thus, 15 percent of the eighty-seven Congressmen interviewed by Davidson, Kovenock, and O'Leary[23] defined their purposive roles (goals) in terms of the formulation of policies for the general welfare; an additional 33 percent defined their duties in terms of floor debate, hearings, investigations, and committee work—all integral parts of the policy process.

In a British parliamentary system, however, the vehicle for translating policy preferences into legislation is, of course, the party. The individual legislator at times may play a supporting role in the drama of policymaking, but it is the party that takes the lead.[24] The question arises as to why a virtually similar proportion of Canadian MPs and American Congressmen (47) percent versus 48 percent) should have structured their purposes essentially in policy terms.

Three reasons suggest themselves. First, as we have shown, these legislators (MPs and Congressmen) have the kind of social backgrounds which are associated with an interest in public policy and the feeling that one is competent to affect policy outcomes.

Second, law making and policy evaluation are functions generally ascribed to all legislators, just as teaching and research are ascribed to all professors. For American Congressmen, such role ascriptions are realistic; for Canadian MPs, they are less appropriate. Just as some professors continue to describe their roles in teaching and research terms when their own experience and the experiences of others indicate that the two tasks are not compatable for all academicians, so we may assume that some legislators in British model parliamentary systems continue to perceive their goals as policy innovation and evaluation even when empirical reality suggests they are no longer appropriate.

Third, the Canadians' concern with policy may be explained in part by a circumstantial variable—the minority position of the Government. The Government leaders, needing the support of every member of their parliamentary group on want of confidence motions, may have been unusually receptive to the policy suggestions of their back benchers. This might account for some of the interest in policy displayed by some members of the Conservative party. The members of the two minority parties,[25] as they frequently kept the Conservatives in office with their votes on crucial divisions, may have felt that they could influence policy substantively in return for their support.

Finally, the Liberals had increased the proportion of seats they had in the 24th Parliament by 100 percent. From the opening of the 25th Parliament they made continuous determined efforts to topple the minority Government and to force an election which, presumably, they felt they could win. Should this occur, they could look forward, as the new governing party, to implementing certain of their policy preferences. As there also had been a large turnover in Liberal party ranks since 1958, many recently elected Liberal MPs may have felt that in the event of victory, they would be named to Cabinet or parliamentary secretaries' posts, where they could influence policy. Undoubtedly, there are other reasons that affect the goals of Canadian legislators some of which are examined in the next chapter.

## *SUMMARY*

Data concerning the circumstances surrounding the legislators' candidacies showed that a majority were prominent officials in their local party organizations at the time they were nominated. Fully 63 percent of the respondents apparently did not have to face an intraparty fight for their party's nomination. A cross tabulation of position at the time of candidacy with the proportion of contested and uncontested nominations indicated that intraparty struggles were most likely to occur when the aspirants were local party officials; they were least likely to occur when respondents had already won some public office. The largest proportion (34 percent) cited personal predisposition as a motive for becoming a candidate. Fully 22 percent claimed that they really did not want to become candidates but were strongly pressured to stand for office. When asked why they continued to maintain their legislative careers, however, it was apparent that some of these previously reluctant individuals were now quite satisfied with their positions. An interesting finding was that those who were disappointed with their legislative careers were not disproportionately the political innocents who had been recruited by the parties, but were the former local party officials, many of whom had used their positions in the hierarchy or past service to the party to claim the nomination.

Another analysis indicated a relationship between majority and minority party status and motives cited for becoming candidates and staying on in Parliament. Despite the fact that the motives of French-Canadian legislators who were Social Creditors differed sharply from Conservative and Liberal respondents with similar cultural backgrounds, certain assumptions concerning the motives of French-Canadian MPs were not supported by the data.

As for the goals of legislators, it was possible to array these along a continuum ranging from policy-centered goals (47 percent) through policy and constituency-oriented goals (30 percent) to constituency-centered goals (23 percent). It was felt that the proportion of legislators who articulated goals concerned with the formulation or evaluation of policy proposals, although appropriate for a sample of Congressmen, was rather high for a Parliament modeled on the British system.

## Notes

1. In the United States the direct primary has modified the local party's role in the nominating process. As Frank Sorauf has pointed out, however, parties have not been defenseless before the primary. By such devices as preprimary conventions and sanctions applied to nonparty candidates, the local parties still manage to nominate their own candidates. As well, the light vote characteristic of many primary contests helps to insure that a "regular" candidate backed by an organized and cohesive party group usually wins. See Sorauf's illuminating discussion in Frank Sorauf, *Party and Representation* (New York: Atherton Press,. 1963), pp. 95–125.

2. See R. M. Dawson and Norman Ward, *The Government of Canada,* 4th ed. (Toronto: University of Toronto Press, 1963), pp. 480–486.

3. Dawson and Ward, p. 482, point out that in some provinces there have been times when the parties of incumbent legislators automatically readopted them without even the calling of ritualistic conventions.

4. Austin Ranney's recent study of candidate recruitment in Great Britain is a conspicuous exception, as is Henry Valen, "The Recruitment of Parliamentary Nominees in Norway," *Scandinavian Political Studies,* **1** (1966), 121–166.

5. Harold D. Lasswell, *Psychopathology and Politics* (Chicago, Ill.: University of Chicago Press, 1930).

6. Frank Sorauf, p. 104, reports that 62 percent of the 212 Pennsylvania legislators and defeated candidates he studied in 1958 encountered no opposition in a party primary.

7. Twelve of the eighteen represented constituencies were very competitive (on the basis of electoral data). The remainder represented moderately competitive districts.

8. The tendency to use a position in local party organizations as a springboard to Parliament is also quite common in another British model parliamentary system, that of New Zealand. See Therese May, "New Zealand Parliamentary Discipline," *Political Science,* **17** (March, 1961), 46. Here it is pointed out that New Zealand MPs "are almost always long-time members of the electoral party and in the vast majority of cases owe their initial selection to active work in and for the party."

9. Austin Ranney, *Pathways to Parliament* (Madison, Wis.: University of Wisconsin Press, p. 72.

10. Ranney, p. 143.

11. Ranney, p. 107–108. That this assumption was not unrealistic is suggested by Henry Valen. His data show that 60 percent of the local Norwegian party leaders whom he studied said that the following qualities were requiring by aspiring candidates for the Norwegian parliament: knowledgeable, experienced from public office, and well known. See Valen, p. 124

12. Heinz Eulau, *Expectations,* p. 121.

13. See Angus Campbell, Philip Converse, Warren Miller, and Donald Stokes, *The American Voter* (New York: John Wiley & Sons, Inc., 1960). Gabriel Almond and Sidney Verba, *The Civic Culture* (Princeton, N.J.: Princeton University Press, 1963), found that these associations exist outside of the United States.

14. Some of these may have been the "power-aspiring careerists," a minority of whom Samuel Eldersveld feels are to be found in any party organization. See Samuel J. Eldersveld, *Political Parties: A Behavioral Analysis,* (Chicago, Ill.: Rand McNally & Company, 1964), pp. 272–303. Eldersveld distinguished between Detroit party activists who were motivated by the need to satisfy personal needs

and who thus saw party work as "personally instrumental," and those who became involved for the purpose of "group realization," (public service, party-oriented, and so forth). If our respondents' motives were to be classified in this way, the "personal predispositions" category would be termed personally instrumental motives, and our "policy-service" and "ideological" categories would qualify for the group realization label.

15. There was, in fact, a correlation of 0.58 between contested and uncontested candidacies and initial recruitment by party as apposed to other agents.

16. Peter H. Rossi and Phillips Cutright, "The Impact of Party Organization in an Industrial Setting," in Morris Janowitz (ed.), *Community Political Systems* (New York: The Free Press, 1961), pp. 81–116, stated that the disadvantaged Republicans found considerable difficulty in recruiting party workers in Gary, Indiana. Key had earlier pointed out that in one-party areas the minor party has great difficulty while the major party can be rather selective in their recruiting.

17. Only three of the fifteen were politically inexperienced when they became candidates. The other was in the "public office" category.

18. For a report of research that indicates that American party leaders have distinct ideological beliefs see Herbert McCloskey *et al.*, "Issue Conflict and Consensus among Party Leaders and Followers," *American Political Science Review*, **54** (1960), 406–427. That the members of parties in Congress have coherent belief systems is suggested by Philip E. Converse, "The Nature of Belief Systems in Mass Public," in David Apter (ed.), pp. 206–261. See, particularly, Tables 7 and 8, pp. 228–229.

19. See Chapter 2 of this book.

20. A legislator's position on the index was determined by coding "2" for every French characteristic he possessed (Catholicism, and so forth) and "0" if he did not possess a trait. If the information had not been ascertained, the interviewee was coded "1," on the assumption that it was equally probable he did or did not possess a particular characteristic. No special weighting scheme was employed, and a legislator's responses simply were summed, and cutting points were established arbitrarily. Legislators were arrayed along a dimension ranging from those who possessed none of these characteristics (position A), to those who had all of them (position D). There were also two intermediary positions—position B in which the respondents have virtually none of the characteristics, and position C in which they have virtually all of them. At times we will combine legislators of positions A and B, and compare them with those of positions C and D. We will also contrast the two polar groups (positions A and D) with the combined intermediary positions (positions B and C).

21. It may appear that the legislators have been arbitrarily assigned to the "mixed" and "area" categories on the basis of some rather fine distinctions. It should be noted, however, that the responses of the former group indicate some direct and explicit concern with legislative policy. On the other hand, the goals of the latter group are oriented either solely toward a specific geographic area or to certain social groups in that area. While the attainment of such area-oriented goals ultimately may require the enactment of legislation, there were no direct references to legislative policies in their responses.

22. There are numerous empirical studies that have been carried out in the United States which illustrate that although party is an important determinant of congressional atitudes and voting behavior, other variables (notably constituency, interest groups, personal predispositions, and so forth) also affect that behavior. Perhaps the most sophisticated attempt to treat the multidimensional aspects of congressional attitudes and behavior is the aforementioned research of Warren

E. Miller and Donald E. Stokes, "Constituency Influence in Congress," *American Political Science Review,* **47** (1963), 45–57. See also Charles F. Cnudde and Donald J. McCrone, "The Linkage Between Constituency Attitudes and Congressional Voting Behavior," *American Political Science Review,* **60** (1966), 66–72.

23. See Davidson, Kovnock, and O'Leary, *Congress in Crisis: Politics and Congressional Reform* (Belmont, Calif.: Wadsworth, 1966), p. 74. The most frequently (40 percent) articulated purposive role was that of "tribune," an orientation very similar to the area orientation of Canadian MPs. Another 8 percent were "brokers," those who saw their jobs as balancing competing interests that strive for policy advantages. The principle concern of the other 4 percent was being re-elected.

24. Robert N. Kelson's study of another British model parliamentary system led him to conclude that the average New Zealand MPs role in the policymaking process is indeed a limited one. See Robert N. Kelson, *The Private Member of Parliament and the Formation of Public Policy: A New Zealand Case Study* (Toronto: University of Toronto Press, 1964).

25. According to Peter C. Newman, an informal and secret agreement had been reached between certain Conservative cabinet ministers and Mr. Robert Thompson, the Social Credit leader, that the government would agree to some Social Credit fiscal policy demands in return for that party's continuous support for the remainder of the parliamentary session. See Peter C. Newman, *Renegade in Power The Diefenbaker Years* (Toronto: McClelland and Stewart, Ltd., 1963).

# 5

# The Correlates of Legislative Goals

Concomitant with the attempt by political scientists to analyze political phenomena in more sophistocated terms, has come a tendency to rely increasingly on sociological and psychological variables as explanations of political behavior. Under the impetus of trying to provide more parsimonious descriptions of the political system, scholars such as Angus Campbell[1] and his colleagues have explained voting preference largely in terms of the strength of individual psychological identification with a political party. Sociologist Seymour Lipset[2] has traced the impact of a sociological variable (social class) upon political behavior; Berelson[3] and his associates have tried to link the social correlates of voting and political participation to a revised theory of democracy. Donald Matthews,[4] on the other hand, has tried to increase our understanding of the composition and functions of elites by an analysis of their social backgrounds.

Of necessity, this desire to provide a parsimonious description has meant that sometimes powerful descriptions of particular aspects of political life have had to be sacrificed. Nevertheless, this strategy not only has added immeasurably to our body of political knowledge, but it has brought to the attention of the more traditional scholars in political science the fact that political institutions do not stand in splendid isolation from the social systems of which they are a part.

Considerations of parsimony have also affected our attempts to test the theoretical notion that legislative role orientations and behavior are the products of initial expectations held for the legislative position; they interact with attitudes and perspectives developed in response to the expectations and requirements of the legislative system. This forces us to explain variations in the goals and representational roles of Canadian MPs in terms of prior and postlegislative incumbency variables. Of necessity, we have not been able to employ every variable that might explain existing goal and representational role variations, but rather have concentrated on variables whose explanatory powers have been demonstrated in previous research. Generally, we have relied on sociological variables to explain variations that may be conceived as functions of the legislators' experiences prior to becoming MPs, and upon psychological variables to explain the impact of factors that we assume become particularly salient once the individuals actually take office.

The prior experience variables we have employed are: position on a French-Canadian Cultural Index, position on a Political Environment Index, position on a Cosmopolitan-Rural Index,[5] education, socioeconomic background (as measured by father's primary occupation), prior political office experience, primary occupation, and motive for becoming a candidate.

The variables that presumably become particularly salient after the individual becomes an actual incumbent are: party affiliation, metropolitan and other constituency differences,[6] perceptions of political competition,[7] contact with constituents,[8] and parliamentary experience.

It already has been noted that most Canadian MPs, because of their activity in party organizations, are probably intensely partisan when they are elected to office. However, we have assumed that there are dimensions of party affiliation that become meaningful to an individual and that affect his role perceptions only after he actually becomes a member of the legislative party. Similarly, the fact that most Canadian MPs live in or have spent a considerable part of their lives in the constituencies they represent, obviously means that the constituencies are important reference objects for them when they come to Parliament. However, actually representing a constituency in a national legislature ought to have some additional impact upon their roles as legislators. It is because we assume party and constituency take on new meaning for the individual *after* he becomes an incumbent of the legislative position that we have included them in the second cluster of variables.

We first will examine the relationship between the several independent variables and legislators' goals. Then, through multivariate analysis, we will try to order the independent variables in terms of their net effect upon the goals of these legislators. Finally, their goals will be employed as an independent variable, to determine whether they are associated with other aspects of legislative behavior such as attitudes toward and contact with interest groups.

## THE IMPACT OF CERTAIN PRIOR EXPERIENCES ON THE GOALS OF LEGISLATORS

As was the case with the respondents' motives for becoming candidates and for staying on in Parliament, we were interested in using the data to test another aspect of the culturalist theory of behavior, specifically, that legislators with French-Canadian cultural characteristics have goals that are structured in terms of their constituencies rather than in terms of the formulation and consideration of legislative policies. We found, when goals were cross-tabulated with the legislators' positions on the French-Canadian Cultural Index, there was but a weak correlation between these two variables (see Table 5.1). Even if one compares only the goals of

TABLE 5.1 GOALS BY POSITION ON FRENCH-CANADIAN CULTURAL INDEX (percentage)

| *Goals* | *French-Canadian Cultural Index Positions* | | | |
|---|---|---|---|---|
| | Position A | Position B | Position C | Position D |
| Policy | 46 | 59 | 43 | 36 |
| Mixed | 26 | 18 | 49 | 34 |
| Area | 28 | 23 | 8 | 30 |
| | ($N$ = 42) | ($N$ = 44) | ($N$ = 35) | ($N$ = 44) |
| | | Gamma = 0.06 | | |

the two groups of legislators at either end of the continuum, the correlation is still an unimpressive 0.10. If the cultural variable is trichotomized and the Position B legislators (those with virtually no French cultural characteristics) and the Position C legislators (those with virtually all the characteristics) are combined and compared with the A and D groups, the resulting correlation is 0.07. Finally, if the A and B legislators are combined in a group, and their goals are compared with the Cs and Ds, the correlation is still 0.03. Nor were there any meaningful relationships (other than education and motives for candidacy) between the other prior experience variables we employed and variations in the goals expressed by the respondents (see Table 5.2).

TABLE 5.2 RELATIONSHIPS BETWEEN LEGISLATORS' GOALS AND CERTAIN PRIOR EXPERIENCE VARIABLES

| *Legislators' Goals* | *Influencing Variables before Incumbency* | *Gamma* |
|---|---|---|
| Goal x | Motives for becoming a candidate | 0.29 |
| Goal x | Educational differences | 0.20 |
| Goal x | Positions on Political Environment Index | 0.09 |
| Goal x | Positions on Cosmopolitan–Rural Index | 0.06 |
| Goal x | Socioeconomic background (fathers' occupation) | 0.02 |
| Goal x | Prior political office experience | 0.15 |
| Goal x | Occupations | 0.04 |

Education is a variable that frequently has been associated with sharp differences in political behavior. As has been indicated, a number of empirical studies have established the fact that political interest, participation, and perceptions of political efficacy increase with education.[9] Thus, the finding that legislators with a college or university degree were somewhat more policy-oriented (49 percent versus 42 percent) and less constituency-oriented (20 percent versus 29 percent) than their colleagues who did not hold degrees was not unexpected. What was intriguing, was the fact that among the better educated respondents, forty-six who had taken some or all of their higher education outside the province in which they grew up were considerably more policy-oriented (62 percent versus 40 percent) than were the more parochially educated. There was, in fact, a correlation of 0.36 between articulated goals and a local or cosmopolitan higher education.

As for the other promising relationship (that between goals and motives for becoming a candidate) one would assume that individuals motivated to become candidates by considerations of policy, service, or ideology would be more likely to have policy-oriented goals than those whose motives were personal. The data indicated there was such a tendency among the interviewees (see Table 5.3). On the whole, however, it was disappointing not to find relationships between variations in the legislators' goals and factors in their preparliamentary backgrounds. There are three possible explanations for the failure of the expected relationships to materialize. First, it

TABLE 5.3 GOALS BY VARIATIONS IN MOTIVES FOR CANDIDACY (percentage)

| *Goals* | *Policy–Service–Ideological Motivation* | *Other Motivation* |
|---|---|---|
| Policy | 55 | 39 |
| Mixed | 29 | 32 |
| Area | 16 | 29 |
| | ($N$ = 75) | ($N$ = 90) |
| | Gamma = 0.29 | |

may have been an unfortunate choice of independent variables. It well may be that if other variables (such as age differences) had been selected to illustrate the effect of experiences prior to incumbency upon goals, correlations would have occurred. Second, the categories of our independent variables (for example, occupation) may not have been sufficiently discriminating. If they had been refined or restructured their use might have proved more rewarding. Third, it may be that Canadian MPs structure their goals largely in terms of the popular pervasive belief that the primary function of legislators is to make laws. Thus, variations in the political, ethnic, and religious milieus in which they were raised in no small part were irrelevant as goal determinants.

Our choice of postincumbency variables, while they did not correlate as strongly with differences in goals as we would have liked, proved to be somewhat more appropriate for explaining variations in the dependent variable. Thus, for example, we found that goals varied with a left-wing (Liberal and NDP) or right-wing (Conservative and Social Credit) party affiliation. In virtually all the analyses that follow, we have combined the members of the two parties on the left of the political continuum and compared them with the parliamentary delegations of the two parties on the right. This strategy was motivated in great part by a pragmatic consideration—the small size of the Social Credit ($N$ = 23) and New Democrat ($N$ = 13) samples. However, the decision can be justified on theoretical grounds as well. It already has been suggested that over the years there has been an ideological convergence between the Liberal and New Democratic parties, and the Conservative and Social Credit parties (to a lesser extent as Conservatives still regard Social Credit monetary theories as unrealistic). Data we have tend to support this assumption. Thus, there were few meaningful differences in the ideological positions taken by Liberals and New Democrats on selected policy issues. Nor did the Conservative and Social Credit MPs differ much in their attitudes. There were, however, very distinct differences apparent when the Liberals and New Democrats were combined and compared with the Conservatives and Social Creditors. Insofar as their goals were concerned, the latter two parties were more inclined than were the former to structure their goals in constituency terms (see Table 5.4). Variations in goals also were correlated (Gamma 0.27)

TABLE 5.4 GOALS BY LEFT-WING AND RIGHT-WING PARTY AFFILIATION (percentage)

| *Goals* | *Left-Wing Parties* | *Right-Wing Parties* |
|---|---|---|
| Policy | 53 | 41 |
| Mixed | 31 | 29 |
| Area | 16 | 30 |
| | ($N$ = 76) | ($N$ = 89) |
| | Gamma = 0.24 | |

with the frequency with which respondents interacted with constituents. Those who visited their districts at least once a week, who received office visits from constituents, who were phoned by constituents, and who received fifty or more letters a week from constituents tended to be more constituency-oriented (33 percent versus 20 percent) and less policy-oriented (35 percent versus 49 percent) than colleagues who had fewer such interactions. Legislators who represented constituencies outside metropolitan areas also tended to express less policy-oriented (43 percent versus 57 percent) and more constituency-oriented goals (26 percent versus 14 percent). However, the goals articulated by Canadian MPs appear to be unrelated to the length of their parliamentary tenure (Gamma = 0.10). Nor was the competitiveness of legislative districts, whether objectively or subjectively measured, correlated with variations in expressed goals (see Table 5.5).

This was rather surprising as conventional wisdom has long held that constituencies exercise a substantial control over their legislative representatives. Because this assumption has rested almost entirely upon impressions, rather than evidence, quantitatively oriented political scientists have tried to subject the legislator–constituency relationship to empirical analysis. Most often, they have tried to demonstrate that variations in legislators' attitudes and behavior are related to differences in the demographic and political characteristics of the constituencies they represent. Generally, this has been accomplished either by cross-tabulating the demographic characteristics of legislative districts or by cross-tabulating the differences in the political competitiveness of constituencies with legislators' roll call votes on policy issues.[10]

TABLE 5.5 A COMPARISON OF THE RELATIONSHIP BETWEEN LEGISLATORS' GOALS AND CONSTITUENCY POLITICAL COMPETITION, OBJECTIVELY AND SUBJECTIVELY EVALUATED (percentage)

| GOALS | OBJECTIVE COMPETITION | | |
|---|---|---|---|
| | *Noncompetitive* | *Moderately Competitive* | *Very Competitive* |
| Policy | 41 | 50 | 49 |
| Mixed | 34 | 32 | 27 |
| Area | 25 | 18 | 24 |
| Total | 100 | 100 | 100 |
| | ($N$ = 46) | ($N$ = 47) | ($N$ = 72) |
| | | Gamma = 0.06 | |
| | PERCEPTIONS OF COMPETITION | | |
| Policy | 48 | 46 | 46 |
| Mixed | 38 | 32 | 29 |
| Area | 14 | 22 | 25 |
| Total | 100 | 100 | 100 |
| | ($N$ = 15) | ($N$ = 58) | ($N$ = 92) |
| | | Gamma = 0.04 | |

To measure the social and political characteristics of legislative constituencies, investigators normally have employed the census and electoral data available to them. Thus, constituencies have been carefully classified in terms of such variables as relative urbanism, the proportion of homes owned or rented, the proportion of white and colored constituents, and the rate at which parties share office during a certain time period.[11]

There are, of course, both pragmatic and theoretical reasons why political scientists have relied almost exclusively upon such measures. First, interested scholars have been able to make use of inexpensive, easily accessible, and generally reliable census and electoral data. Second, it seems theoretically justifiable to assume that legislators in democratic societies will be encouraged, if not compelled, to represent the dominant socioeconomic interests of their constituencies because of the periodic and constitutionally enforced possibility that they might be removed from office. Political competition with its potential sanction of defeat may be seen as the mechanism that constituents employ to influence the behavior of their legislative representatives. We have tried to test this latter notion by cross-tabulating the goals and representational roles of Canadian MPs with the competitiveness of their constituencies.

Since both goal selection and representational role-taking are highly subjective cognitive processes, however, it was felt that a measure of political competition based upon the respondents' own perceptions of their legislative districts would be more likely to delineate the influence of this factor upon them than more objective measures based on electoral or census data.[12] (In the next section, we shall present data which suggest that our attempt to delineate the relationship between a legislator's role orientation and his perception of how competitive is his district was not entirely in vain.)

To recapitulate, analysis has indicated that a Canadian MP expresses goals that can be arrayed along a policy-constituency continuum. In part, variations in these goals can be explained by the interaction of prior experience variables (such as education and motives for candidacy) with variables such as left-right party affiliations or relative urbanism of constituencies. The latter variables, it has been suggested, become particularly salient once an individual becomes an incumbent of the legislative position. This interaction can be rather interestingly illustrated by the use of an additive model. For example, 47 percent of the sample expressed policy goals. If we look at the goals of only individuals with ideological and policy motives, the proportion who were policy-oriented rises to 53 percent. If we isolate individuals who, in addition to expressing ideological–policy motives, also had college educations, we find 76 percent of them articulating policy goals. Another arrangement would isolate left-wing party members (with college educations) who had infrequent contacts with constituents in their metropolitan area districts. In such a group we found the proportion who express policy goals has risen from 47 percent to 83 percent. In other words, the more variables we add which seem to make a legislator policy-oriented, the greater the probability he will express policy goals; the same generally is true if we cumulate those variables that are associated with an area orientation.

Although such an additive model illustrates the fact that different combinations of independent variables affect legislators' goals, it does not tell us which variable is most important, in the sense that it is most strongly related to variations in goals. One method of discerning this would be to examine, in turn, the relationships between each of the independent explanatory variables and the dependent goals while holding constant the other independent variables. If we do this, however, we very quickly run out of cases. (For example, when we tried to examine the relationship between a right-wing party affiliation and variations in goals, while holding constituency and educational differences constant, in one instance we were left with a cell with an *N* of five.)

A second problem is that our independent variables are, themselves, frequently related. When, for example, we look at the relationship between variation in goals and education, the gross relationship between these two variables involves some spurious elements "built in" by the correlation between educational differences and other independent variables such as social background.

There is available a computer program (the Multiple Classification Analyses)[13] which *does* permit the user to assess the net effect of each of a number of predictor variables upon the dependent phenomenon while taking into account the second problem mentioned above, interaction. However, one of the assumptions underlying the program is that the data are of the equal interval variety. That is, there ought to be equal distances such as three, six, and nine between the categories. As these data did not fulfill this requirement, we made only experimental use of the program, so that we at least could *suggest* which independent variables appeared to be related most strongly to variations in legislators' goals and representational roles.

The only surprises that resulted from this analysis were the attrition of the relationship between goals and representing a metropolitan or nonmetropolitan constituency (Tau Beta[14] = 0.08), and the increased magnitude of the correlation between goals and positions on the French-Canadian Cultural Index. The attrition of the correlation between goals and relative urbanism of constituencies suggests that in great part it was spurious, manifesting an association between goals and other independent variables with which metropolitan and nonmetropolitan constituencies also are related. The increase in the magnitude of the correlation between goals and differences in the legislators' cultural backgrounds (as measured by their positions on the French-Canadian Cultural Index) is more difficult to explain. As a check, we used position on the French-Canadian Cultural Index in combination with differing clusters of variables. Consistently, position on the index, education, and left-right party affiliations were the best predictors of variations in goals. The explanation for the fact that the data previously indicated a relationship between variations in goals and the variables of education and party affiliation, but not with position on the index would seem to lie in the theoretical nature of the relationships depicted by the Multiple Classification Analysis. The program generates correlations uncontaminated by the presence of other variables. Thus, in and of itself, a French Canadian, as opposed to someone of another cultural background, is associated with differences in articulated goals. In the Canadian House of Commons, however, a French cultural background or lack of it is but one of a vast number of factors that interacts and acts upon the MP. In these interactions the influences of education and party apparently were strong enough to be manifested overtly, while ethnic and religious cultural influences upon legislators' goals were submerged by more pressing concerns.

Thus, the culturalist theory (insofar as legislators' goal selection is concerned), would appear to be in error, not in its contention that French-Canadian cultural characteristics influence legislative behavior, but rather that such characteristics make all other influences to which the legislator is subjected, irrelevant.

## THE RELATIONSHIP BETWEEN LEGISLATIVE GOALS AND OTHER BEHAVIOR

Until now we have shown that the goals expressed by Canadian legislators can be arrayed along a continuum, and that variations in goals are associated with differences in their backgrounds and party affiliations. The question arises as to whether differences in the goals they express really matter; that is, are they associated with other differences in their attitudes and behavior? To aid in answering this question we will employ the respondents goals' as the independent variable, and then cross-tabulate them with other aspects of behavior; specifically, these other aspects are: differences in the motives expressed for maintaining a legislative career, differences in attitudes toward constituents, differences in contacts with and attitudes toward interest groups, and differences in behavior in hypothetical conflict situations.

It will be remembered that there was a continuum underlying the legislators' motives for maintaining a legislative career that ranged from those who said they would have no regrets about terminating their stay in Parliament, through those who wanted to stay on because of service, policy, and ideological considerations, to those who expressed motives that were personally instrumental (such as psychological gratification derived from interaction with congenial peers). A cross tabulation of motives for maintaining a parliamentary career with legislators' goals revealed that the proportion of respondents citing personal predispositions motives increased from 33 percent to 61 percent as one went from the policy to the area end of the goals continuum. If we extract the legislators who had mixed goals, and look only at respondents with policy or area goals (in each group comparing the proportions with policy, service, and ideology as opposed to personal predisposition) the differences are sharper, with the correlation rising from 0.25 to 0.56.

In studying members of four American state legislatures, Heinz Eulau[15] found that those who took "tribune" purposive roles (analogous to area-oriented goals) generally tended to feel more efficacious and less frustrated than the "inventors" (an orientation analogous to policy-oriented legislators). What may be a related finding is that our constituency-oriented MPs tended to perceive less conflict, as measured by their positions on a Constituency Conflict Index,[16] between their constituents and themselves than did the others (see Table 5.6). Again, if we extract the legislators who expressed

TABLE 5.6 Relationship between Positions on a Constituency Conflict Index and Goals (percentage)

| *Conflict Index* | *Goals* | | |
|---|---|---|---|
| | Policy | Mixed | Area |
| Much conflict | 32 | 18 | 10 |
| Some conflict | 21 | 25 | 24 |
| No conflict | 47 | 57 | 66 |
| | ($N$ = 78) | ($N$ = 49) | ($N$ = 38) |
| | | Gamma = 0.27 | |

mixed goals, the correlation between the two variables is increased, rising from 0.27 to 0.37.

Differences between policy-oriented and area-oriented legislators also extended to their attitudes toward and, particularly their contacts with interest groups.[17] There was a correlation of 0.21 between goals and attitudes toward interest groups. Whereas 54 percent of respondents with a policy interest were favorably disposed toward interest groups, only 33 percent of the more parochially oriented shared this attitude. More striking were the differences in contacts with interest groups related to goal variations (see Table 5.7). To us, these data suggest that Canadian MPs with a real desire to evaluate and initiate legislative policies probably find that communications with interest groups facilitate the realization of this goal. Although his counterpart in the United States Congress often laments, with justification, his paucity of staff assistance,[18] the Canadian MP, unless he is of

TABLE 5.7 Relationship between Contact with Interest Groups and Goals (percentage)

| *Interest Group Contact* | *Goals* | | |
|---|---|---|---|
| | Policy | Mixed | Area |
| Frequent contact | 42 | 20 | 13 |
| Occasional contact | 49 | 67 | 74 |
| No contact | 9 | 13 | 13 |
| | ($N$ = 78) | ($N$ = 49) | ($N$ = 38) |
| | | Gamma = 0.38 | |

Cabinet rank, has no staff assistance whatsoever apart from a single stenographer-typist. The information he might normally have had access to (if he had a staff) is lacking; in this respect, interest groups may well serve as the functional equivalents of staff in the Canadian parliamentary system.[19] The data they supply him may assist the MP in intelligently evaluating and discussing a particular piece of legislation either in caucus or, should the occasion arise, on the floor of the House. One can speculate that interest group representatives may even, in certain instances, provide the legislator with a cause for which he can labor. We have already pointed out that the average back bench member of a parliamentary system plays a rather limited role in initiating or substantively influencing policy proposals that become law. This is a function largely preempted by the Government party. However, sufficient information from interested groups, and the motivation to act in a systematic and sustained way on this information may increase the probability of the individual MP having his needs for initiating policy met. Interest groups may provide the members with data that can become the basis of either a question or policy proposals for the government. Assuming that there is sufficient time and popular support, the proposal might even become law through the medium of a "private member bill." Unfortunately, to date, there have been no empirical studies[20] that might validate these speculations.

Finally, the data also show that in one instance goal differences appear to be related to the cues MPs will accept in hypothetical conflict situations. The interviewees were first asked the following question: "If you wanted to take a certain stand on an issue before the House, but felt that the majority of the people in your constituency would want you to take a different stand, what would you probably do?" Their responses indicate that 22 percent probably would be guided by constituency opinions; 42 percent would try to effect some sort of reconciliation between constituency views and their own, generally by trying to convince the constituency of the correctness of their positions,[21] and 36 percent would take the position that *they* believed to be right regardless of constituency opinion. The latter group of legislators tended to have policy goals while the largest proportion of those who said they would abide by the wills of their constituents were to be found among the MPs with constituency-centered goals (see Table 5.8). The magnitude of the correlation is increased to 0.57 if we remove the mixed goals group of legislators and compare only those with policy and area interests. Interestingly, this kind of distribution did not occur when the hypothetical conflict was not between respondents and their constituents, but between the legislators' parties and constituencies. In fact, a substantial proportion of Canadian MPs were unable to even conceptualize such a conflict. Their initial response to the question, "If you felt the majority of your constituents were opposed to your party's stand on a

TABLE 5.8 RELATIONSHIP BETWEEN STANCE ON POLICY ISSUES AND GOALS (percentage)

| *Policy Issue Stance* | *Goals* | | |
|---|---|---|---|
| | Policy | Mixed | Area |
| Ignore constituency views | 50 | 30 | 19 |
| Reconcile constituency | 37 | 47 | 44 |
| Opinion guided by constituency views | 13 | 23 | 37 |
| | (*N* = 78) | (*N* = 49) | (*N* = 38) |
| | | Gamma = 0.41 | |

legislative issue, how would you probably vote on the issue?" were "I don't think this could ever happen but . . ." or "I doubt that this would occur but. . . ." Others said that they would try very hard to be away from Parliament on the day that such a vote was scheduled. When pressed to make a choice, the responses of 50 percent were that they would make some attempt to reconcile party and constituency opinion. Most said they would visit their constituencies, and in a series of meetings explain their party's position. Others said they would work in party caucus to get the party, rather than the constituency, to change their views. However, the proportions who would vote with the party or in support of their constituents were not appreciably different among policy-mixed or area-oriented MPs (see Table 5.9).

TABLE 5.9 RELATIONSHIPS BETWEEN VOTING ON A LEGISLATIVE ISSUE AND GOALS (percentage)

| *Legislative Issue Voting* | *Goals* | | |
|---|---|---|---|
| | Policy | Mixed | Area |
| Vote with party | 34 | 36 | 28 |
| Reconcile | 50 | 49 | 52 |
| Vote against party | 16 | 15 | 20 |
| | (*N* = 78) | (*N* = 49) | (*N* = 38) |

Our interpretation of these data is that they offer another illustration of how large the legislative party looms in the world of a legislator in a British model parliamentary system.[22] The reluctance of the majority of legislators with constituency-centered goals to vote against their party suggests that they, no less than the others, regard the party as the mechanism through which their demands, however parochial, are most likely to be realized. If this interpretation is valid, and the aspirations of most Canadian MPs *are* linked with the activity and success of their legislative party, they are afforded another motive for acting in concert with party colleagues. It well may be, as Leon D. Epstein[23] has suggested:

> The individual legislators of a governing (or potentially governing) party have an entirely rational motivation for cohesion in a parliamentary system that they do not have under the separation of powers. Each parliamentary vote on an important policy issue involves the question of whether the MP wants a cabinet of his party or of the opposition. Thus each vote becomes a party vote in a sense politically meaningful to the individual MP. He has a dominant motivation to support his party on each such vote. . . . In Canada, as in Britain, the parliamentary system provides this motivation regularly rather than only occasionally as in the United States. It is a motivation that, except in the most extraordinary instance, transcends the disagreements which are bound to exist among MPs of a given party especially in a nation as diverse as Canada.

## *SUMMARY*

The data indicated that the goals of Canadian MPs could be arrayed along a continuum ranging from those who were interested exclusively in the formation and evaluation of legislative policy, through those who combined a policy orientation with a more parochial interest in their constituency, to those whose aspirations were focused entirely upon their constituencies. It was hypothesized that their goals were determined by prior experience variables interacting with factors that became particularly salient after the respondents actually became MPs. Analysis indicated that variations in education, motives for becoming candidates for office, left–right party affiliations, and the relative urbanism of the constituencies they represented all were related to differences in goals expressed by the respondents. The use of an additive model showed that isolating legislators, in terms of characteristics associated with particular goals, increased the proportion of these goals. Experimental use was made of the Multiple Classification Analysis program to suggest which of our independent variables might in themselves be the best predictors of legislators' goals. Variations in education, party, and position on the French-Canadian Cultural Index exhibited the strongest net relationships with variations in goals, while the correlation with relative urbanism was sharply attenuated, suggesting it largely was spurious.

Finally, we employed goals as an independent variable and found that they could be meaningfully related to different motives for maintaining a legislative career, attitudes toward and contact with interest groups, position on a Constituency Conflict Index, and the extent to which a legislator would accept constituency over his own policy preferences in the event of a conflict. Interestingly, variations in goals *were not* related to a willingness to accept either party or constituency cues in the event of a difference between the two. These data were interpreted as affording one measure of the importance of party in a British model parliamentary system.

## Notes

1. Angus Campbell *et al., The American Voter* (New York: John Wiley and Sons, Inc., 1960).

2. Seymour M. Lipset, *Political Man* (New York: Anchor Books, 1963).

3. Bernard Berelson, Paul F. Lazarsfeld, and William McPhee, *Voting* (Chicago, Ill.: University of Chicago Press, 1954). See also Paul F. Lazarsfeld, Bernard Berelson and Hazel Gaudet, *The People's Choice* (New York: Duell, Sloan and Pierce-Meredith Press, 1944).

4. Donald R. Matthews, *The Social Background of Political Decision-Makers* (New York: Random House Inc., 1954).

5. This index was intended to capture the influence of residence in an urban or rural environment upon the interviewees. A "cosmopolitan" legislator was raised in a city rather than on a farm, in a village, or in a small town; he had never spent any appreciable time (six years) in a rural area, and was neither a farmer nor the son of a farmer. A "provincial" legislator was one whose primary occupation was that of a farmer. He was the son of a farmer, had been born on a farm, and had spent over six years in a rural environment. The "semi-provincial" legislator had shared some of the experiences of his provincial colleagues. The correlations among the four variables that comprised the index ranged in strength from 0.79 to 0.96.

6. As a belief long cherished by political scientists is that cleavage between urban and rural elements in a society underlies a substantial proportion of political conflict, we intended to classify the legislative constituencies in terms of their proportion of urban dwellers. Originally, forty-two sample constituencies were extracted which were wholly within metropolitan areas, such as Toronto, Montreal, Vancouver, and Winnipeg. The remaining districts were then classified as "rural" if 51 percent of the population did not live in population enclaves of 1000 or more, and semirural if they did. Thus, 49 percent of the constituencies were classified as rural, 25 percent as semirural, and 26 percent as metropolitan. Further consideration led us to abandon this classification because we came to believe that most of the semirural districts were essentially rural in nature, with the large enclaves of population set in the midst and servicing the needs of surrounding farms, mining, or timber areas. Had most of the dependent variables in this study been of the equal interval or ratio variety, relative urbanism could have been treated as a linear and continuous variable by classifying each constituency in terms of a ratio (expressed in percent) of some arbitrary number of urban dwellers over the total population therein. As the dependent variables were ordinal, we decided upon a Metropolitan–Other dichotomy.

7. This subjective measure of interparty competition was based upon responses to the question, "How about the strength of the parties in your constituency? Would you describe your constituency as very competitive, moderately competitive, or not competitive?"

8. This is a composite measure based upon responses to questions on how

frequently legislators visited their constituencies, the amount of mail they received from constituents, and the extent to which constituents communicated with them by phone or personal visits to Ottawa.

9. See, particularly, the work of Angus Campbell *et al.,* The American Voter (New York: John Wiley & Sons, Inc., 1960.) However, the nineteenth century liberal political theorists such as Alexis de Tocqueville, *Democracy in America* (New York: Vintage Books, 1954), and John Stuart Mill, *On Liberty and Consideration of Representative Government,* R. B. McCallum (ed.) (Oxford: Oxford University Press 1946), both pointed out the relationship between an educated population and the success of liberal-democratic institutions. Lord Bryce pointed out that "education, if it does not make men good citizens, makes it at least easier for them to become so." James Bryce, *South America: Observation and Impressions* (New York: The Macmillan Company, 1912), p. 546. Educator and philosopher John Dewey went further in that he saw education as the basic requirement of democracy. John Dewey, *Democracy and Education* (New York: The Macmillan Company, 1916).

10. See the late Julius Turner, *Party and Constituency: Pressure on Congress* (Baltimore, Md.: Johns Hopkins University Press, 1951), and Duncan MacRae, "The Relation Between Roll Call Votes and Constituencies in the Massachusetts House of Representatives" in Heinz Eulau *et al.* (eds.), *Political Behavior: A Reader in Theory and Research* (New York: The Free Press, 1959), pp. 317–329. See also Lewis Froman, *Congressmen and Their Constituencies* (Chicago, Ill.: Rand McNally & Company, 1963) and Heinz Eulau, "The Legislator and His District: Area Roles" (particularly pp. 291–299), in John Wahlke, Heinz Eulau, William Buchanan, and Leroy Ferguson, *The Legislative System* (New York: John Wiley & Sons, Inc., 1962), pp. 287–311.

11. See, for example, Froman, *Congressmen and Their Constituencies;* Heinz Eulau, "The Ecological Basis of Party Systems: The Case of Ohio," *Midwest Journal of Political Science,* **1** (1957), 125–135; David Gold and John Schmidhauser, "Urbanization and Party Competition: The Case of Iowa," *Midwest Journal of Political Science,* **4** (1960), 62–75; and Phillips Cutright, "Urbanization and Competitive Party Politics," *Journal of Politics,* **25** (1963), 552–564. A rather elaborate classification of congressional districts, in terms of their competitiveness, also is contained in Malcolm Moos, *Politics, Presidents, and Coattails* (Baltimore, Md.: John Hopkins Press, 1952). For a review of much of the literature in this area see Norman Meller, "Legislative Behavior Research," *Western Political Quarterly,* **13** (1960), 131–153, and "Legislative Behavior Revisited," *Western Political Quarterly,* **18** (1965), 776–794.

12. A comparison of the two measures suggests that Canadian MPs tend to view their constituencies as more politically competitive than a classification based on electoral data would suggest. For example, over one quarter of the legislative constituencies that on the basis of voting returns could reasonably be classified as not competitive, were viewed as very competitive by their representatives in Parliament. Further, over one half of the constituencies classified as only moderately competitive were seen as very competitive. Nevertheless, there was a correlation of 0.56 between their own evaluations and the evaluation based upon the electoral data. We also tried to construct a subjective measure of the social characteristics of their constituencies. Thus, the legislators were told, "Of course, constituencies will differ a good deal in terms of their economic, social, ethnic, occupational and religious characteristics. From this point of view, what are the important features of your district?"

Although the respondents had experienced little difficulty classifying their constituencies in terms of their competitiveness, they experienced considerable difficulty with the second question. Over 30 percent could not respond in any meaningful way. Even the probe, "What would you say is the most characteristic feature of your constituency?" elicited relatively meaningless replies such as: (1) "It's heterogeneity." (2) "The people are hard-working and decent" and (3) "It's plain honest people." The responses that were meaningful were also so varied and presented such a monumental coding problem that to date we have not undertaken the task.

13. This is also known as the Lippet Iterative Program. I am indebted to Professor David Goldberg of the University of Michigan for acquainting me with this program. For a detailed discussion of the statistical techniques employed in this program see James Morgan *et al., Income and Wealth in the United States* (New York: McGraw-Hill, Inc., 1962), Appendix E.; and Donald E. Pelz and Frank Andrews, *The SRC Computer Program for Multivariate Analysis: Some Uses and Limitations* (Ann Arbor, Mich.: Survey Research Center, 1961). For empirical studies that employed this program see Harold Wilensky, "Mass Society and Mass Culture: Interdependence or Independence," *American Sociological Review,* **29** (April 1964), 173–179; and Michael T. Aitken, "Kinship in an Urban Community," (Doctoral dissertation, University of Michigan, 1964).

14. The magnitude of the Tau Beta correlations normally is less than that of the Tau Gamma statistic used elsewhere.

15. Heinz Eulau, "The Legislator as Decision Maker: Purposive Roles," in John Wahlke *et al., The Legislative System* (New York: John Wiley and Sons, Inc., 1962), p. 264.

16. The data are derived from responses to five questions. The legislators were asked whether they felt "the majority of their constituents feel the same way about this (a civil liberties issue, a welfare issue, and a foreign policy issue) as you do?" They were also asked whether there were differences between what they wanted to accomplish (their goals) and what their constituents wanted, and between their conceptions of what the legislative position entailed and their constituents' conceptions. For each item, respondents who answered "no" or no with a slight qualification were scored "0"; those who answered "yes" and "no" (that is, they perceived differences with some constituents but not with others) were scored "1"; and those who answered "yes" or yes with a slight qualification were scored "2." Intercorrelations were computed, respondents' scores were cumulated, and cutting points were established arbitrarily so that legislators were arrayed along a dimension ranging from those who perceived "much conflict," through those who saw "some conflict," to those who felt there was "no conflict" between their constituents and themselves over selected policy issues and the interpretation of the legislative role.

17. To measure orientations toward interest groups the respondents were asked, "How often do pressure groups contact you as an MP?" and "What do you think of these attempts by pressure groups to contact you as an MP?"
There were three codes for the frequency of contact: "frequent" (once a week or more), "occasional" (less than once a week), and "never."

There were also three codes for attitudes toward interest groups: "pro" (favorable or favorable with slight reservation), "neutral" (neither favorably nor unfavorably disposed), and "anti" (unfavorable or unfavorable with slight reservations).

18. Michael O'Leary (ed.), *Congressional Reorganization: Problems and Projects: A Conference Report* (Hanover, N.H.: Public Affairs Center, Dartmouth College, 1964), pp. 22–23. Congressional requests for increased staff assistance

have been supported by congressional scholars such as James A. Robinson. See James A. Robinson, "Decision Making in Congress," in Alfred de Graza (ed.), *Congress: The First Branch of Government* (Washington: American Enterprise Institute for Public Policy Research, 1966), pp. 259–296.

19. In their study of four American state legislatures wherein "staff" is in similarly short supply, John Wahlke and his associates found that a large proportion of their respondents justified the attention they gave to the interest groups in just such functional terms. According to Wahlke,

> Legislators' comments on the usefulness of interest groups show that their own conceptions of groups' functional utility include the inclusion of "technical information" described by Truman. But legislators frequently went beyond this to admit a general readiness to use lobbyists as briefing agents who save legislators' time by doing some of their research work for them.

See "The Legislator and the Interests: Pressure-Group Roles," in Wahlke *et al.*, p. 338.

20. There are, however, a number of good descriptive studies available dealing with the operation of interest groups in a British parliamentary system. See John Millet, "The Role of an Interest Group Leader in the House of Commons," *Western Political Quarterly,* **9** (1956), 915–926; Samuel Beer, "Pressure Groups and Parties in Britain," *American Political Science Review,* **50** (1956), 1–23 J. D. Stewart, *British Pressure Groups: Their Role in Relation to the House of Commons* (Oxford: University Press, 1958); and S. E. Finer, *Anonymous Empire: A Study of the Lobby in Great Britain* (London: Pall Mall, 1958).

21. The views of these respondents were remarkably similar to the "mentor" attitude Heinz Eulau found among American State legislators. The mentor orientation appears to combine both a desire to take into account constituency opinion and a paternalistic view that constituents' minds can be changed by educating them as to what is the proper position to take. Thus, Eulau reported that American mentors maintained communications with constituents so that they could persuade and convince them and bring them around to their convictions. See Heinz Eulau, "The Legislator and his District: Areal Roles," p. 307.

22. We are afforded another illustration of this phenomenon if we contrast the distribution of attitudes among Canadian MPs with those of the Pennsylvania state legislators studied by Frank Sorauf. Sorauf categorized his legislators once on the district versus area judgment conflict and also on their general ranking of constituency, party, and their own judgment in their overall concept of the legislative role. Of 105 legislators, 47 percent were constituency-oriented, 26 percent regarded their own judgment as most important, 20 percent wanted to reconcile conflicting opinion, and *only 9 percent* ranked the party first. See Sorauf, pp. 123–124. If we take an average of their replies to the two hypothetical conflict questions we find that in contrast only 16 percent of Canadian MPs rank the constituency first; 46 percent would try to reconcile divergent opinions (the mentor orientation); 36 percent would rely on their own judgment; and fully 33 percent would rank the party first. Insofar as resolving a hypothetical self versus constituency conflict, the proportion of Pennsylvania state legislators who would take constituency cues was somewhat larger than we found (39 percent versus 22 percent) while only 28 percent of the Americans as compared to 42 percent of the Canadians would try to reconcile differences between constituents and themselves.

23. Leon D. Epstein, "A Comparative Study of Canadian Parties," *American Political Science Review,* 58 (1964), 46-59.

# 6

# The Correlates of Representational Roles

In a penetrating analysis of Edmund Burke's famous Speech to the Electors of Bristol, Heinz Eulau argued that it was necessary to distinguish analytically between the style and focus of the representative process in any empirical study of representation.

Burke postulated two possible foci of representation:

> local, necessarily hostile interests, on the one hand; and a national interest on the other hand . . . . But in doing so, he also linked these foci of representation with representational styles. If the legislator is concerned with only one interest, that of the whole, and not with compromise among diverse interests, it follows that the representative cannot be bound by instructions, from whatever source, but must be guided by what Burke called "his unbiased opinion, his mature judgment, his enlightened conscience."

As will be indicated shortly, the remarkable influence that Burke's antithetical proposals have had is manifested by the fact that, although the proportions differed considerably, the legislators in our sample (the American state legislators studied by Eulau, and the American Congressmen studied by Davidson and his colleagues) all tended to perceive the representational function in these general terms.

## REPRESENTATIONAL ROLES

Representational style may be conceptualized as the manner in which a legislator carries out his perceived functions, while focus is the geographic area that he perceives he represents. To determine how the legislator carries out his perceived functions the respondents in this study were asked, "What do you think your representational role entails?" To ascertain the answer to this the following question was put: "Some MPs feel that their primary responsibility is first to their constituency and then to their province or country as a whole. Others feel quite differently. How do you feel about this?" Responses to the first query indicated that the legislators could be arranged along a bidimensional consultation–service continuum of representational role styles ranging from those who felt that they were required neither to consult with nor perform services for their constituents, through those who tried to combine some consultation and service with a degree of independence from the constituency, to those who sought constantly to consult with and perform services for constituents. The first and smallest group have been termed "trustees." Like their spiritual mentor Edmund Burke, they claimed to be virtually free agents who acted in terms of their perceptions of the national interest and common good. A response typical of this small group of legislators was: "Fundamentally, to do as good a job as I can for the country with the opportunity available, I act according to my conscience. The alternative is to toady to voters and I never will."

A second and larger group of legislators who will be termed "politicos,"[2] apparently tried to span the chasm between independent thinking and behaving, and constituency influence and control. Although most of them acknowledged or accepted the necessity of consulting constituents and performing services for them, they also agreed that a degree of independence from the constituency was a requisite for effective representation. A response typical of the group was: "It entails fighting for what I think is right. It also entails being a representative of the people of my constituency. I accept the fact that I have to deal with their problems, but I also have to fight for the integrity of Parliament and for a program of social legislation."

Finally, the remaining 49 percent of the respondents, whom we term "delegate–servants," justified their role styles in functional terms. That is, they felt that their positions *required* them to consult and seek advice and also to perform any services requested from them. A typical response was: "It entails being a sounding board for constituency opinion, and then making it known. A great many people feel helpless in solving their problems if they have to do with government. After all, government is so big, that the average person is simply lost in the maze. So they turn to their MP to open doors to proper authorities, and you become the link between the public and the administrative offices. Many people who have grievances would never get a hearing without an MPs help."

Insofar as their focus of representation was concerned, the largest group of respondents perceived the nation as the geographic area to which they owed primary responsibility. A second group perceived their constituencies as being of primary importance, while the remainder could not or would not articulate a preference for any particular geographic area. We have termed the first orientation "national," the second one "local," and the third one "national–local." Responses typical of each of these orientations, respectively, were: "My primary responsibility is to the nation"; "My first duty is to my constituency. They are the ones who elected me"; "I can't see why these are imcompatible. I am elected to serve the country, but this is not and has not ever been inconsistent with serving my constituency and its people, nor do I see why it should be."

As one would suspect, variations in representational role styles were associated with differences in foci of representation, although the relationship is not as strong as the one revealed by a cross tabulation of similar data for American state legislators (0.36 versus 0.55).[3] The latter, insofar as the distribution of their role *styles* was concerned, fit Burke's model of the good legislator far better than do American Congressmen or Canadian MPs. On the other hand, state legislators are more parochial in their foci than are either group of national legislators[4] (see Table 6.1).

One explanation for the existence of these differences may be inferred from Miller and Stokes' informative discussion of representation. First, however, it should be noted that the data in Table 6.1 support the Miller and Stokes assumption that neither the instructed delegate nor the independent trustee is a realistic model of the representational relationship. Thus, approximately one-quarter of the state legislators, a third of the MPs, and fully one-half of a sample of American Congressmen articulated a role style that combines elements of both the delegate and trustee models. In their analysis, Miller and Stokes[5] point out that, although they usually are conceptualized as being diametrically opposed, both the responsible party and instructed delegate theories of representation share the notion of popular control, the difference being that in the former the controller is conceived in terms of a national rather than a local constituency. In

TABLE 6.1 A COMPARISON OF THE REPRESENTATIONAL ROLE STYLES AND FOCUSES OF REPRESENTATION OF CANADIAN MPs, AMERICAN CONGRESSMEN,[a] AND STATE LEGISLATORS[b] (percentage)

| | *Canadian MPs* | | *American Congressmen* | | *State Legislators* |
|---|---|---|---|---|---|
| Representational Style | | | | | |
| Trustee | 15 | | 28 | | 63 |
| Politico | 36 | | 50 | | 23 |
| Delegate | 49 (Delegate–servant) | | 20 | | 14 |
| | ($N$ = 165) | | ($N$ = 116) | | ($N$ = 295) |
| Representation Focus | | | | | |
| National | 47 | National | 30 | State | 25 |
| National–local | 19 | National–local | 28 | State–local | 30 |
| Local | 34 | Local | 35 | Local | 45 |
| | ($N$ = 165) | | ($N$ = 116) | | ($N$ = 283) |

[a] Data for congressmen are derived from R. Davidson, "Congress and the Executive," p. 394. Columns do not total 100 percent because of unclassified respondents.

[b] Data for state legislators are derived from *The Legislative System*, p. 291 and p. 308.

responsible party systems, candidates for national office appeal to the electorate in terms of a national party program and leadership to which, if elected, they will be committed.

It seems reasonable to assume that in comparison to his counterpart in Congress and, assuredly in American state legislatures, the Canadian MP stands at the most responsible end of a responsible party continuum; he (far more than do the others) *does* campaign on a national party platform and he *is* pledged to support the policies and leaders of his party. Again, more than do the others, he feels the constraints imposed on his behavior by both party and constituency. Thus, he tends to focus on a geographic area other than his constituency; generally shuns an orientation that is structured in terms of independence from party and constituency; and finds, because he plays only a limited part in the policy process, that the role of delegate-servant is both a congenial and efficacious one.

This is not to suggest that there were not other and perhaps more compelling reasons for the large proportion of delegate-servants and the relatively miniscule group of trustees found in this legislative body. One of these may have been the large number of competitive rural constituencies found in Canada. The Multiple Classification Analysis again will be employed to suggest how the role correlates ought to be ordered, and finally, as was the case with their goals, representational role orientations will be used as an independent variable to ascertain whether variations in roles taken are related to other aspects of legislative behavior.

## REPRESENTATIONAL ROLE-TAKING

Of the prior experience variables, only education and primary occupation appeared to have any impact upon representational roles. The chief differences in representational role styles taken by college graduates and those who were not college graduates was that the majority (69 percent) of those who were not college graduates preferred the delegate–servant orientation (Gamma = 0.39). They also tended to focus upon their constituencies more (42 percent versus 30 percent) than did their better educated colleagues (Gamma = 0.21).

As was the case with the goals they expressed, college–cosmopolitan respondents differed somewhat from their less traveled but equally educated colleagues in that a smaller proportion of the former took delegate-servant orientations (45 percent versus 34 percent) and were more nationally focused (57 percent versus 45 percent). Occupation was related to representational styles (Gamma = 0.25) rather than to representational foci (Gamma = 0.02). Legislators who had been businessmen or professionals prior to becoming MPs tended to take a trustee role *more* frequently (18 percent versus 7 percent), and the delegate–servant role *less* frequently (47 percent versus 58 percent) than legislators who had been farmers or who had worked at low status blue and white collar jobs prior to their election.

Again, the data fail to support the extreme culturalist assumptions that French-Canadian legislators are excessively parochial in their outlook, and disproportionately prefer the delegate–servant role style. In fact, to the extent that there is a relationship between a French-Canadian cultural background and representational role orientations, it is in the direction opposite to that predicted by the culturalists (see Table 6.2).

Apart from education and occupation, there were no relationships between representational role differences and the prior experience variable employed in our analysis. Again, however, as with their goals, post incumbency variables more frequently were associated with differences in the dependent variable. For example, representing a metropolitan constituency appeared to be correlated with a tendency to take *other* than a delegate–servant role style and to focus upon the nation rather than the constituency (see Table 6.3). Whereas variations in their goals had been unrelated to the competitiveness of their districts (whether the competition was measured objectively or subjectively), we found representational role styles, but not foci, related to their perceptions of interparty constituency competition (see Table 6.4).

TABLE 6.2 REPRESENTATIONAL ROLES BY POSITIONS ON THE FRENCH-CANADIAN CULTURAL INDEX (percentage)

| | *French-Canadian Cultural Index* | | | |
|---|---|---|---|---|
| | Position A | Position B | Position C | Position D |
| Representational Style | | | | |
| Trustee | 14 | | 29 | 23 |
| Politico | 46 | 36 | 33 | 28 |
| Delegate–servant | 40 | 64 | 38 | 49 |
| | | Gamma = −0.06 | | |
| Representational Focus | | | | |
| National | 47 | 43 | 43 | 55 |
| National–local | 14 | 21 | 29 | 16 |
| Local | 39 | 36 | 28 | 29 |
| | ($N$ = 42) | ($N$ = 44) | ($N$ = 35) | ($N$ = 44) |
| | | Gamma = −0.08 | | |

TABLE 6.3 RELATIONSHIP BETWEEN REPRESENTATIONAL ROLES AND REPRESENTING A METROPOLITAN OR NONMETROPOLITAN CONSTITUENCY (percentage)

| | *Metropolitan Constituency* | | *Nonmetropolitan Constituency* |
|---|---|---|---|
| Representational Style | | | |
| Trustee | 23 | | 12 |
| Politico | 40 | | 35 |
| Delegate–servant | 37 | | 53 |
| | | Gamma = 0.30 | |
| Representational Focus | | | |
| National | 63 | | 41 |
| National–local | 22 | | 19 |
| Local | 15 | | 40 |
| | | Gamma = 0.45 | |
| | ($N$ = 42) | | ($N$ = 123) |

The findings that represented a nonmetropolitan area constituency or one perceived by the incumbent as being very competitive (both associated with a tendency to take the delegate–servant rather than the trustee role style), suggested that these tendencies would be increased in districts that combined the two characteristics; that this was indeed the case was not

TABLE 6.4 THE RELATIONSHIP BETWEEN REPRESENTATIONAL ROLES AND POLITICAL COMPETITION, SUBJECTIVELY AND OBJECTIVELY EVALUATED (percentage)

SUBJECTIVE COMPETITION

| | *Noncompetitive* | *Moderately Competitive* | *Very Competitive* |
|---|---|---|---|
| Representation Style | | | |
| Trustee | 41 | 15 | 11 |
| Politico | 32 | 38 | 36 |
| Delegate–servant | 27 | 47 | 53 |
| | | Gamma = 0.24 | |
| Representational Focus | | | |
| National | 61 | 40 | 48 |
| National–local | 20 | 34 | 11 |
| Local | 19 | 26 | 41 |
| | | Gamma = 0.12 | |
| | ($N$ = 15) | ($N$ = 58) | ($N$ = 92) |

OBJECTIVE COMPETITION

| | *Noncompetitive* | *Moderately Competitive* | *Very Competitive* |
|---|---|---|---|
| Representational Style | | | |
| Trustee | 22 | 13 | 11 |
| Politico | 34 | 33 | 40 |
| Delegate–servant | 44 | 54 | 49 |
| | | Gamma = 0.09 | |
| Representational Focus | | | |
| National | 49 | 51 | 43 |
| National–local | 26 | 17 | 16 |
| Local | 25 | 32 | 41 |
| | | Gamma = 0.14 | |
| | ($N$ = 46) | ($N$ = 47) | ($N$ = 72) |

particularly surprising (Gamma = 0.40). What was rather surprising was that ninety-four constituencies could be classified as rural and very competitive. These data tend to support Howard Scarrow's study of Canadian electoral behavior. Scarrow[6] found that Canadian rural constituencies, in contrast with United States constituencies, were more competitive and had higher voter turnouts than urban constituencies.

One wonders why Canada should differ from the United States in these respects. One suggestion is that this difference may be explained by the substantial proportion of rural congressional districts in the United States that lie in the Solid South, an area disproportionately attached to the

Democratic party. An important finding by Angus Campbell[7] and his colleagues is that a psychological identification with a party tends to stabilize interparty competition; associated with a party identification is a tendency to regularly vote for a party regardless of the contents of the party's program or the visibility of the positions of the party's candidates on policy issues. They also found that outside the South, the farmer tends to be less strongly identified with a party; his turnout at elections is less predictable, and he is a less stable partisan than an urban dweller. This kind of volatile political behavior increases interparty competition, as there is less probability that the voter will vote for the party he last supported or, indeed, that he will vote at all. Alternately, a substantial number of persons who did not participate in one election may turn out to vote against the incumbent in another election. If this is the behavior of American farmers in areas in which there is more than a single party for which to vote, we may infer that such behavior is even more likely to occur in Canadian rural districts in which there are not two but, frequently, four parties from which the voter can choose. Thus, one explanation for the presence of such a large proportion of highly competitive rural constituencies in Canada is that so many are not one-party but, rather, four-party areas.

It will be remembered that historian William Morton claimed that the Progressive party, although short-lived, had important effects on subsequent Canadian political behavior; the traditional partisan attachments (Liberal and Conservative) of the electorate were seriously weakened, and two new parties emerged to compete for national and local office. In a recent article, Howard Scarrow[8] went beyond this to claim that Canadians are not strongly identified with *any* of the parties and, in fact, that they generally have a weaker party identification than Americans. A cursory examination of recent aggregate statistics tends to support Scarrow's thesis; they show that the level of support received by the four Canadian parties fluctuates much more than does the support received by the Republican and Democratic parties (see Table 6.5). Thus, a second reason for the presence of so many competitive rural districts and, if we may extrapolate, for the generally high level of interparty competition and resultant large turnover in the House of Commons membership, is relatively weak identification of the Canadian electorate with their parties. Carrying the analysis a step further, the Canadian MP (faced with an electorate for which a party label is not too meaningful and which, particularly in rural areas, is not intensely loyal), may find that a parochial role orientation, in part predicated on performing services for individuals or groups in his constituency, is both an appropriate and judicious choice. Regardless of how rational the choice of these roles may be, the members of the two left-wing parties tended to find a delegate–servant role style and the constituency focus less congenial orientations than did the right-wing MPs (see Table 6.6). A

TABLE 6.5 COMPARISON OF THE AVERAGE VOTES AND FLUCTUATIONS IN THE VOTES OF PARTIES IN CANADA AND THE UNITED STATES (percentage)

| *Level of Support* | CANADA | | | | UNITED STATES | |
|---|---|---|---|---|---|---|
| | *Social Credit* | *Conservative* | *Liberal* | *New Democratic Party* | *Republican* | *Democrat* |
| Average vote[a] | 5.0 | 35.5 | 43.4 | 11.8 | 47.7 | 50.6 |
| Average fluctuation | 2.4 | 6.5 | 5.7 | 2.0 | 1.9 | 2.4 |

[a] Average vote in Canada is for seven national elections between 1940 and 1962. In the United States, it is for eleven elections between 1940 and 1960.

TABLE 6.6 REPRESENTATIONAL ROLE STYLES BY LEFT-RIGHT PARTY AFFILIATIONS (percentage)

| | *Left-Wing Parties* | | *Right-Wing Parties* |
|---|---|---|---|
| Representational Style | | | |
| Trustee | 21 | | 11 |
| Politico | 46 | | 26 |
| Delegate–servant | 33 | | 63 |
| | | Gamma = 0.47 | |
| Representational Focus | | | |
| National | 57 | | 39 |
| National–local | 21 | | 18 |
| Local | 22 | | 43 |
| | | Gamma = 0.34 | |
| | ($N$ = 76) | | ($N$ = 89) |

partial explanation for this may lie, of course, in the fact that the Conservative MPs, as their party leaders were temporarily the heads of the several ministries, had better access to the machinery that could satisfy constituent demands. Thus we might find in some future study of the Canadian House of Commons that a governing party of the left also would find a parochial representational role orientation more attractive than the above data suggest. Or, it may have been the fact that the Government was in a minority and thus faced the possibility of a defeat and another appeal to the electorate that accounted for the Conservative's parochialism. If this *was* the case, the tapping of grass-roots opinions and, particularly, the building of constituency good will by performing services may have been perceived as entirely rational behavior by a party wishing to be re-elected.

The Quebec campaign of the Social Creditors (the other right-wing party) featured the charges that the two old parties had failed to articulate the interests of the people.[9] Thus, they may have interpreted their unexpected victories in twenty-six Quebec constituencies as a mandate to focus on their constituencies and to take the delegate–servant role style.[10]

Further, a larger proportion of right-wing respondents represented rural and nonmetropolitan constituencies. Thus, it could be argued that their parochial role orientations were inspired as much by a desire to be re-elected as by party ideology. Since variations in representational role styles and foci of representation also were correlated (Gamma = 0.22 and 0.56, respectively) with differences in the length of parliamentary experience, it was felt that the Multiple Classification Program would be particularly useful in suggesting which of these variables were the best predictors of representational roles.

When the program was applied to the data, we found that a right-wing or left-wing party affiliation was most strongly associated with representational role style variations. It should be noted, however, that this may not have been an entirely fair test for the perception of political competition variable. As only fifteen respondents perceived their constituencies as noncompetitive, we hesitated to employ perception of competition as a predictor variable. In the single instance in which it was grouped with party affiliation and metropolitan and other constituency representation it was second to party (0.25 versus 0.18 Beta) as a predictor of variations in role styles.

As was the case with the goals that legislators articulated, position on the French-Canadian Cultural Index had a considerably stronger net relationship to variations in role style than was previously indicated. However, the impact of French cultural characteristics on differences in foci of representation was less strong. Interestingly, educational differences also were fairly strongly correlated with role styles, and less strongly associated with foci of representation. The representational foci of the respondents were most strongly correlated with differences in parliamentary experience, a left-wing or right-wing party affiliation, and the representation of a metropolitan or other constituency.

In our concluding section we will try to explain the anomalous relationships between goals, representational role orientations, and French cultural characteristics when the data are subjected to multivariate analysis. For the present, it should be noted that, unlike the situation with representational styles, the net relationship between party affiliation and representational focus was not clearly the strongest, as the magnitude of the correlation fluctuated with different combinations of variables. However, it was consistently the first or second best predictor. Although our data do not meet the requirements of the Multiple Classification Analysis program, a multivariate analysis has suggested that, on the whole,[11] a left-wing or right-wing affiliation is most strongly correlated with variations in the goals expressed and the representational roles taken by Canadian MPs. Representational roles will be used as an independent variable to ascertain whether variations in roles are associated with other aspects of legislative behavior.

## DO DIFFERENCES IN REPRESENTATIONAL ROLES MATTER?

Although motives for becoming candidates for Parliament were not related to variations in representational roles, the respondents' motives for maintaining a legislative career *were* so correlated. The trustees and politicos were moved by ideological-policy-service motives more often than were delegate–servants. The latter tended to cite what have been termed personal predispositions, as did those whose foci of representation were their constituencies (see Table 6.7). Interestingly, the nationally focused legislators were

TABLE 6.7 RELATIONS BETWEEN MOTIVES FOR SUSTAINING A LEGISLATIVE CAREER AND GOALS (percentage)

| WHY SUSTAIN CAREER | REPRESENTATIONAL ROLE STYLE | | |
|---|---|---|---|
| | *Trustee* | *Politico* | *Delegate–Servant* |
| Not motivated | 9 | 9 | 9 |
| Policy–service–ideological | 72 | 53 | 41 |
| Personal predisposition | 19 | 38 | 50 |
| | ($N$ = 26) | ($N$ = 58) | ($N$ = 81) |
| | | Gamma = 0.28 | |
| | | REPRESENTATIONAL FOCUS | |
| Not motivated | 11 | 9 | 5 |
| Policy–service–ideological | 56 | 44 | 42 |
| Personal predispositions | 33 | 47 | 53 |
| | ($N$ = 78) | ($N$ = 32) | ($N$ = 55) |
| | | Gamma = 0.29 | |

no more sustained by ideological aspirations than were legislators with a more limited focus of representation, but a substantially larger group of trustees cited purely ideological motives for maintaining careers (37 percent versus 19 percent and 13 percent).

The Burkean trustees also were different in that a larger proportion (33 percent versus 21 percent) were in the "much conflict" position of the constituency conflict index as compared with the others. Conflict perceptions also were associated (Gamma = 0.30) with foci of representation in that the nationally focused tended to see more conflict.

There was no relationship between representational role differences and either contact with interest groups (Gamma = 0.11 and 0.02) or attitudes toward these groups (Gamma = 0.04 and 0.06). However, variations in representational roles generally were related to differences in cue-taking in hypothetical conflict situations involving the constituency, on one hand, and personal and party positions on the other. For example, those individuals who were at once both nationally and locally focused (in keeping with their double orientations) were more inclined than others to reconcile any differences. As we would expect, the locally focused and the delegate–servants were the most proconstituency, but even these legislators were more willing to accept their constituents' positions if the latter conflicted with

TABLE 6.8 RELATION BETWEEN CUE-TAKING IN THE EVENT OF CONFLICT AND REPRESENTATIONAL ROLES (percentage)

| LEGISLATORS' STANCE | REPRESENTATIONAL ROLE STYLE | | |
|---|---|---|---|
| | *Trustee* | *Politico* | *Delegate–Servant* |
| Constituency versus Personal Position | | | |
| Ignore constituency | 50 | 36 | 33 |
| Reconcile | 43 | 47 | 38 |
| Guided by constituency | 7 | 17 | 29 |
| | | Gamma = 0.24 | |
| Constituency versus Party Position | | | |
| Vote with party | 39 | 33 | 32 |
| Reconcile | 48 | 52 | 48 |
| Vote against party | 13 | 15 | 20 |
| | | Gamma = 0.10 | |
| | REPRESENTATIONAL FOCUS | | |
| | *National* | *National–Local* | *Local* |
| Constituency versus Personal Position | | | |
| Ignore constituency | 45 | 30 | 28 |
| Reconcile | 45 | 57 | 28 |
| Guided by constituency | 10 | 13 | 44 |
| | | Gamma = 0.38 | |
| Constituency versus Party Position | | | |
| Vote with party | 41 | 23 | 29 |
| Reconcile | 49 | 68 | 42 |
| Vote against party | 10 | 9 | 29 |
| | | Gamma = 0.28 | |

their own wishes than if they conflicted with party positions (see Table 6.8). Still, we found that 16 percent of the members of a British model responsible party legislative system indicated that they would vote against their party, although the conflict between party and constituency was hypothesized rather than actual. Conventional wisdom holds that cohesive party action is the *conditio sine quo non* for the functioning of such a system. The data already have suggested which individuals are most likely to act independently of their party colleagues: the less experienced (from zero to six years of parliamentary tenure), members of the two right-wing parties, and those who represent relatively or completely rural and highly competitive constituencies.

## *SUMMARY*

Examination of the data on the distribution of representational role orientations among the respondents, American Congressmen, and the members of four American state legislatures indicate that in their representational role styles the latter fit Edmund Burke's model of the good representative much better than do Congressmen and, particularly, MPs. However, the Canadians were more nationally-focused than either group of American legislators. When variations in representational role styles were cross-tabulated with certain prior experience variables, only education and primary occupations were correlated with the dependent roles. In general, the better educated and those who had been in the business world or were members of a profession tended to select the less parochial roles. Representational role styles, but not foci of representation, were related to the legislators' perceptions of constituency competition. Relative urbanism of constituencies, length of experience as MP, and left-wing or right-wing party affiliation also affected the representational roles they took.

Despite the fact that there were highly visible differences in roles (which could be attributed to other factors), a multivariate analysis suggested that a left-wing or right-wing party affiliation usually was the best predictor of the representational role orientations taken by Canadian MPs.

Finally, representational role differences were employed as an independent variable. Analysis indicated that they were related to motives for maintaining a legislative career, to perceptions of constituency conflict and, in part, to the positions legislators took in hypothetical conflict situations involving their parties, their constituencies, and themselves.

# Notes

1. Heinz Eulau, "The Legislator as Representative: Representational Roles," in John Wahlke *et al.*, *The Legislative System* (New York: John Wiley & Sons, Inc., 1962), p. 270.

2. The term was first used by Eulau, pp. 267–286.

3. Eulau, p. 396. It should be noted that the data reported are for only 197 of the 474 (41 percent) interviews taken by Wahlke and his colleagues. It may be that the correlation for the Americans would have been of approximately the same magnitude as for the Canadian if the data for the former were complete.

4. There is a correlation of only 0.19 between the national backgrounds of Canadian MPs and American Congressmen and their representational focuses, but one of —0.45 between national background and representational styles.

5. Warren E. Miller and Donald E. Stokes, *"Constituency Influence in Congress," American Political Science Review,* **57** (1963), 45–46.

6. Howard A. Scarrow, "Patterns of Voter Turnout in Canada," *Midwest Journal of Political Science,* **5** (1961), 351–366. Not only were there more very competitive nonmetropolitan sample constituencies when competition was measured objectively (40 percent versus 36 percent), but also when they were subjectively evaluated. Thus, 76 percent of the nonmetropolitan districts which were very competitive were seen as very competitive, but only 63 percent of the very competitive metropolitan districts were perceived as such.

7. Angus Campbell *et al., The American Voter* (New York: John Wiley & Sons, Inc., 1960), pp. 64–167. See also Angus Campbell, Philip E. Converse, Warren E. Miller, and Donald E. Stokes, "Party Government and the Saliency of Congress," *Elections and the Political Order* (New York: John Wiley & Sons, Inc., 1966), pp. 194–211.

8. Howard Scarrow, "Distinguishing Between Political Parties—The Case of Canada," *Midwest Journal of Political Science* (February 1965), 61–76.

9. This claim was similar to the charges made by Social Credit leaders a generation earlier during their first successful provencial campaign in Alberta.

10. Interestingly, the data suggest that performing services may have been perceived, particularly by the members of the right-wing parties, as more important than the tapping of constituency opinions. Thus, for the sample as a whole (and unlike the case with legislators' goals) there was no relationship between variations in representation role styles (Gamma = 0.04) or focuses of representation (Gamma = 0.02), and frequency of interaction with constituents. Nor were there appreciable differences in the proportions of right-wing and left-wing legislators who were "frequent interactors" (25 percent versus 20 percent). However, there were party-related differences in attitudes toward the importance of constituency services. For example, 86 percent of the right-wing members said their constituents thought that the performing of services for them (constituents) was an important part of the MPs job as opposed to 64 percent of the left-wingers (Gamma = 0.37). Further, 69 percent of the right-wingers felt that performing services was important in getting them re-elected as compared to 55 percent of their left-wing adversaries with similar feelings (Gamma = 0.28). On the other hand, in reply to a question asking whether constituents were more interested in services or an MPs position on policy issues, there were negligible differences in their responses (49 percent of right-wingers said their constituents were more interested in services than policy positions as compared with 43 percent of the left-wing members).

11. There may be highly visible differences associated with variables that we have not been able to consider.

# 7

# The Normativeness of Party

According to Heinz Eulau:[1]

> Regardless of whether he is an office holder, a party functionary, or a voter, what we seem to know best about an American's political roles is that he is either a Democrat or a Republican. But party labels, as external symbols of partisan roles, do not seem to involve corresponding expectations concerning behavior appropriate to the labels. There is little consensus on what it means to be a Democrat or Republican.

Among these Canadian legislators, however, there was a fairly strong consensus on what it means to be a member of one of the four national parties in Canada. Their perceptions of their own and the other parties generally coincided with the positions traditionally ascribed to the parties. For example, the Liberal party is regarded as one favoring lower tariffs, welfare measures, provincial autonomy, good relations with the United States, and an accommodation with French Canada. The Conservatives tend to be viewed as the party of Protestant, English-speaking Canada; they are for big business, maintaining close ties with Britain and the other Commonwealth countries, and taking a "hard line" toward French-Canadian aspirations.

The CCF–NDP is regarded as a socialist party pledged to implement those policies one normally ascribes to socialists (welfare state measures, planned economy). Finally, the Social Credit party popularly tends to be seen as a right-wing party—strongly individualistic, conservative in their attitudes toward governmental activity but, at the same time, advocating utopian financial panaceas that certainly would require government action.

To ascertain whether the legislators' impressions of the parties were related to the parties' popular images, they were asked, "Do you think there are fundamental differences among Canadian parties?"

An overwhelming majority (84 percent) did think that there were fundamental differences among the parties. When asked to articulate these differences, some proceeded to cite what were essentially differences in style (such as Social Credit nihilism, Conservative hypocracy, Liberal arrogance, and New Democratic dogmatism). However, 65 percent of the references to the Social Credit party, 60 percent of the Conservative party, 45 percent of the Liberal party,[2] and 75 percent of the citations referring to the New Democrats, *did* describe the parties in many of the same terms used above. As Newcomb, Turner, and Converse[3] have pointed out, however, such a consensus may not really indicate the extent to which attitudes are shared by any group, as the perception of consensus may not be accurate. Thus, in this section we try to determine the extent to which the ideological positions of the parties on selected policy issues actually fit the popular images held of them, and the images they tend to hold of themselves. If they do or, alternately, if the data show that substantial numbers of right-wing and left-wing party members take distinct ideological positions, we may infer that the cohesiveness of Canadian parliamentary parties, in part at least, is facilitated by shared attitudes on policy issues.

With regard to testing whether some of the positions normally ascribed to them were in fact held by the parties, we sought to ascertain whether: (1) right-wing party members were more concerned with individual liberty than left-wingers in a "man versus the state" issue; (2) left-wingers were more in favor of "welfare statism" and increased national government activity than were right-wingers; (3) the positions of right-wingers on a liberal–conservative[4] scale were more conservative, and whether left-wingers were more liberal; and (4) left-wingers were more sympathetic toward French-Canadian aspirations for cultural equality than were right-wingers.

In this section, we also try to determine whether the respondents have distinct attitudes toward their party organizations in the electorate. Specifically, we asked them how big a part and what functions the local party organizations performed in the last electoral campaign. It is felt that these and other data are important additions to the literature because legislative behavior scholars have never ascertained the importance of local party organizations as legislators' reference groups; nor have they determined whether local parties influence the behavior of the legislators they help to elect. On the other hand, they long have been cognizant of the interactions between legislators and such important groups in their role sets as constituents, administrators, and interest groups.

The latter part of this chapter is concerned with the respondents' motives for maintaining party cohesion. We try to suggest why the majority of Canadian MPs, although they apparently are not stringently disciplined, still generally act in concert with their parties.

## IDEOLOGICAL[5] POSITIONS ON POLICY ISSUES: ATTITUDES TOWARD EXTENSION OF CULTURAL DUALISM[6]

The dimensions of political conflict vary over time. However, in this century, three issues have been the subjects of controversy on a fairly regular basis in most Western democracies. These are: the conflict between individual freedom and public authority; the conflict over welfare statism (the use of the power and resources of a national government to redistribute national wealth on a more equitable basis); and the conflict over the continued democratizing of public life, which may be termed the liberal–conservative conflict.

In Canada, an additional and perhaps more crucial dimension of conflict has been that underlying the cleavage between French-Canadian Catholics and English and English-oriented Canadians. This conflict has its roots deep in Canada's history and, in fact, the foundations for a cultural regionalism in Quebec already were present when in 1867 a combination of economic, political, and military factors induced Quebec to enter a federal union that also embraced the provinces of Ontario, Nova Scotia, and New Brunswick. This regionalism was to manifest itself in a nationalist movement which, in this century, has taken such diverse forms as: (1) a desire to sever Canada's ties with Great Britain, the "mother country" for a majority of her citizens; (2) an isolationist tendency that culminated in intense opposition to Canada's participation in the two great wars of this century; (3) sporadic outbreaks of anti-semitism; (4) a claim that Quebec has a special constitutional status not shared by the other nine provinces; and

(5) the growth of a separatist movement that sought to establish Quebec as an independent national and Catholic state.[7]

The most enduring tendency has been an increasingly vocal insistence that Canada has been and always was intended to be a biethnic and bicultural country. Consequently, Canadian social and political institutions ought to reflect these facts. Although Quebec's entrance into the federal union, as well as the Conservative party's long initial dominance of Canadian national politics, rested on an English-Protestant and French-Catholic coalition engineered in that century by Conservative party leaders Sir John A. Macdonald and Sir Etienne Cartier, the Liberal party generally has been regarded as having the most favorable attitude toward French Canada. Indeed, the twenty-two years of uninterrupted Liberal party hegemony was ascribed, in part, to Prime Minister Mackenzie King's sagacity in naming, as his right-hand men in the Cabinet a series of French Canadians, presumably to dramatize Liberal party sympathies for the French Canadian.

It was because Quebec was the Liberal party's functional equivalent of the Solid South that Mr. Gordon Churchill,[8] the chief Conservative strategist, excluded that province from his plans for a Conservative party victory in 1957. Despite the fact that the Conservatives supposedly were anathema to Quebec voters, the latter returned fifty-one Conservatives in the Conservative triumph in 1958. However, in 1962 their representation was reduced to fourteen MPs. In part, this latter attrition may have been related to Liberal leader Lester B. Pearson's unabashed wooing of French-Canadian voters and, in part, to the Conservatives, particularly Prime Minister Diefenbaker and his inept handling of the opportunity afforded him. Support for this latter assumption was gleaned from the responses of French-Canadian Conservative MPs.

At any rate, the replies to the question on the extension of biculturalism reveal that the Conservatives, as a party, were the least favorably inclined to French-Canadian aspirations. However, it was the Social Credit party rather than the Liberal party that was most in favor of these aspirations. The responses to this question, unlike the others, differed so greatly with each party that we present data for all four parties. Among the Liberals and Conservatives (the only parties who had elected representatives from Quebec, Ontario, and the residual areas) the Liberals from the latter two regions were more in favor of biculturalism than were the Conservatives. There was, however, no difference in the proportions of Conservatives and Liberals from Quebec who favored biculturalism. Over-all, the data tend to support the popular and legislators' images of Liberal and Conservative party attitudes toward French Canada. They also show that the majority of the Liberals and Social Creditors shared favorable attitudes toward biculturalism; the majority of the Conservatives were opposed, while the New Democrats were divided on this issue (see Table 7.1).

TABLE 7.1 ATTITUDES TOWARD EXTENSION OF CULTURAL DUALISM BY PARTY AFFILIATION (percentage)

| | PARTY AFFILIATION | | | |
|---|---|---|---|---|
| *Attitudes toward Extension of Cultural Dualism* | *Social Credit* | *Conservative* | *Liberal* | *New Democrat* |
| Favor extension | 80 | 33 | 67 | 42 |
| Against extension | 16 | 64 | 30 | 50 |
| Not ascertained | 4 | 3 | 3 | 8 |
| | ($N$ = 23) | ($N$ = 66) | ($N$ = 63) | ($N$ = 13) |

## A CIVIL LIBERTIES ISSUE

To measure differences in attitudes toward an issue involving the attempted curtailment of certain civil liberties by a government, the respondents were asked an open-end question[9] dealing with a piece of legislation passed by a Quebec provincial legislature. (The legislation had been declared unconstitutional by the Canadian Supreme Court.)[10]

There was an underlying dimension to the responses; these ranged from outright condemnation, through those who felt that the act had both good and bad features, to unreserved approval. A cross tabulation of these attitudes with left-wing and right-wing party affiliations revealed that the right-wing legislators were less opposed to the act than were the left-wing legislators (see Table 7.2). As the act was passed by a French-Canadian

TABLE 7.2 ATTITUDES TOWARD PADLOCK ACT BY PARTY AFFILIATION (percentage)

| | PARTY AFFILIATION | |
|---|---|---|
| *Attitudes toward Padlock Act* | *Left-Wing Parties* | *Right-Wing Parties* |
| Against | 73 | 52 |
| Pro-con | 2 | 14 |
| For | 25 | 34 |
| | ($N$ = 76) | ($N$ = 89) |
| | Gamma = 0.35 | |

provincial legislature, we assumed that the respondents' positions on the French-Canadian Cultural Index would have influenced their attitudes so strongly that they could not be overlooked. Examination of the data indicated that there was such a relationship (Gamma = 0.23), albeit, less strong than was assumed. Further, for the Conservatives and the Liberals (the only two parties who had individuals in all four positions of the index), party differences remained constant. That is, all four groups of Conservative party members were more in favor of the Padlock Act than culturally equivalent groups of Liberals. The data indicate that although the majority of left-wing party members held the same attitude on this issue, the right-wingers were divided. Also, despite the attitude of concern for individual rights and the necessity of safeguarding them from encroachment by government, it would appear from these data and those shown in Table 7.3, that the right-wingers are more concerned with the economic rather than the civil rights of Canadians.

## WELFARE STATISM[11]

As in other Western democracies, the left-wing parties in Canada generally have tended to perform an innovative function, introducing into the political system a majority of the issues whose debatable limits define the grounds on which the political battles have been waged.[12] They also have taken a positive attitude toward the increased scope of activities engaged in by the national government. Thus, we would expect the Liberal and New Democratic legislators (rather than the right-wing parties) to be more in favor of policies designed to redistribute wealth, and to employ the resources of the national government to solve nationwide social and economic problems. Nor did the Liberal and New Democrats disappoint

TABLE 7.3 POSITION ON THE WELFARE STATE INDEX BY PARTY AFFILIATION (percentage)

| | Party Affiliation | |
|---|---|---|
| *Position on Welfare State Index* | *Left-Wing Parties* | *Right-Wing Parties* |
| Strongly favor | 59 | 8 |
| Moderately favor | 35 | 45 |
| Strongly oppose | 6 | 47 |
| | ($N$ = 76) | ($N$ = 89) |
| | Gamma = 0.84 | |

us; their responses showed them to be much more strongly in favor of such items than were the Conservatives and Social Creditors. The result was a very strong positive correlation between position on the Welfare State Index and left-wing or right-wing party affiliation (see Table 7.3).

## POLITICAL PARTICIPATION AND TOLERANCE: A LIBERAL–CONSERVATIVE SCALE

Sixteen "agree-disagree" items were submitted for Guttman scaling.[13] The four items that scaled concerned legislators'[14] attitudes toward the efficacy of interest group action, the power of trade unions, and the rights of individuals holding unpopular political and religious beliefs to publicly express those opinions.[15] Thus, a "liberal" is one who would permit interest groups and unions a role in the socio-political process, and would also allow members of unpopular religious and political groups to participate in decision-making, in that he would not restrict their opportunities to interact with and influence public attitudes. A "conservative" is one who takes the opposite position toward these groups, whereas a "moderate" is one who occupies a middle position between these poles. Again, as might be expected from their popular images, the members of the two left-wing parties tended to be considerably more liberal than the Conservatives and Social Creditors. However, conservative attitudes were more widely shared by the right-wingers than were liberal attitudes by the left-wingers (see Table 7.4).

Although the left-wing and right-wing members of the legislative parties do not quite live up to the attitudes popularly ascribed to them, they do hold fairly distinct attitudes on policy issues. These attitudes generally

TABLE 7.4 RELATIONSHIP BETWEEN POSITION ON A LIBERAL–CONSERVATIVE SCALE AND PARTY AFFILIATION (percentage)

| | PARTY AFFILIATION | |
|---|---|---|
| *Position on Liberal–Conservative Scale* | *Left-Wing Parties* | *Right-Wing Parties* |
| Liberal | 43 | 17 |
| Moderate | 30 | 22 |
| Conservative | 27 | 61 |
| | ($N$ = 73) | ($N$ = 85) |

Gamma = 0.56

are shared by a substantial proportion of each party group and thus may facilitate cohesive action by party members.

## PARTY ORGANIZATION IN THE ELECTORATE

Bowman and Boynton[16] have pointed out that local party organizations frequently have rather staggering tasks assigned to them a priori by party theorists. These include the mobilization of voters, the espousal of the party's ideology, the recruitment of workers and leaders, the dispensing of patronage, and so forth.

Although in the past few years there have been an increasing number of empirical studies of parties as organizations,[17] to the best of our knowledge there have been few, if any, that have studied party organizations from the viewpoint of their most immediate beneficiaries—the ones they elected to public offices.

Responses to the question, "How important was your party organization in determining the outcome of the election?" indicated that the majority of Canadian MPs, regardless of party affiliation, felt that their parties played a crucial role in electing them. Fully 85 percent of the left-wing and 78 percent of the right-wing party members described their local organizations' contributions as very important. When asked what tasks the party actually performed[18] it was clear that, like the party organizations in the two states studies by Bowman and Boynton,[19] the direct canvassing of voters was the most important task performed by local party organizations. Local parties were also active doing committee-room work (making up and mailing party and candidate literature from party headquarters), providing opportunities for candidates to meet their constituents, performing election day chores, and raising campaign funds (see Table 7.5). Although relatively similar proportions of right-wingers and left-wingers reported committee work and fund raising[20] as important activities, it was evident that the left-wing party organizations were considerably more active in directly contacting voters or enabling the candidates to have face-to-face contacts with voters. On the other hand, right-wing local party organizations were more active in performing what might be termed administrative tasks (committee work, election day work, and fund raising). If we label the former " direct contact work" and the latter "indirect contact work" we find a correlation of 0.34 between type of local party activity and left–right party affiliation.

After a lead-in question concerning their awareness of constituency opinions on policy issues the interviewees were asked, "How do you make sure about the accuracy of the information you get?" The responses revealed that local right-wing party organizations seem to be more important reference groups for their legislative representatives than do left-wing constitu-

TABLE 7.5 MOST IMPORTANT TASK PERFORMED BY LOCAL PARTY ORGANIZATIONS (percentage)

| | Party Affiliation | |
|---|---|---|
| *Task Performed* | *Left-Wing* | *Right-Wing* |
| Canvass voters | 38 | 28 |
| Committee work[a] | 20 | 21 |
| Help candidates meet voters[b] | 18 | 10 |
| Election-day work[c] | 8 | 22 |
| Raise and provide funds | 9 | 8 |
| Nothing or practically nothing (no other reply) | 7 | 11 |
| | (*N* = 76) | (*N* = 89) |

[a] Prepare and mail out literature.
[b] Arrange formal meetings, coffee, and cocktail parties.
[c] Baby-sit, provide transportation, check polls for irregularities.

ency organizations. In addition to local party organizations, the MPs also cited local newspapers, returns from mailed questionnaires,[21] and their own interaction with constituents as sources of information. Approximately 14 percent of the respondents said that it was difficult or impossible to ascertain opinions with any degree of accuracy. Another 10 percent said that they knew *intuitively* what constituents' opinions were. However, they refused to elaborate when probed for the bases of their insight (see Table 7.6). If nonparty sources are combined and compared with party sources

TABLE 7.6 SOURCES FOR DETERMINING THE ACCURACY OF INFORMATION CONCERNING LEGISLATIVE DISTRICTS (percentage)

| | Party Affiliation | |
|---|---|---|
| *Sources for Determining Accuracy of Information* | *Left-Wing* | *Right-Wing* |
| Contacts with local party leaders and workers | 46 | 69 |
| Local newspapers | 14 | 7 |
| Polls (mailed questionnaires) | 7 | 4 |
| Intuition | 15 | 7 |
| Very difficult | 16 | 12 |
| Not ascertained | 2 | 1 |
| | (*N* = 76) | (*N* = 89) |

we find a correlation of —0.42 between a left–right party affiliation and the employment of local party organizations (as opposed to other sources) as reference groups. In view of this, it was somewhat surprising that when the respondents were asked to rank their sources,[22] *there was little difference* (Gamma = 0.09) in the proportions of left-wingers and right-wingers who cited local party people as the source that provided the most accurate information concerning constituency feelings (see Table 7.7).

TABLE 7.7 MOST ACCURATE SOURCES OF INFORMATION BY PARTY (percentage)

| | PARTY AFFILIATION | |
|---|---|---|
| *Most Accurate Sources of Information* | *Left-Wing* | *Right-Wing* |
| Local party leaders and workers | 46 | 41 |
| Business leaders | 10 | 21 |
| Local union officials | 4 | 1 |
| Local religious officials | 4 | 7 |
| Local ethnic leaders | 6 | 2 |
| Personal friends and neighbors | 14 | 10 |
| Depends on the issue[a] | 16 | 18 |
| | ($N$ = 76) | ($N$ = 89) |

[a] The legislators in this category claimed it was impossible to ascribe to any single group or individual the accolade of "best" informant, as the knowledge and competence of most groups and individuals almost always is limited to a particular area.

Taken together, the data contained in Tables 7.6 and 7.7 suggest that local party organizations constitute important reference groups for legislative incumbents. Because party activists are likely to view the world of the constituency through partisan blinkers, Canadian MPs, particularly members of the two right-wing parties, probably get a somewhat biased sampling of constituency opinions. That the right-wingers recognized this possibility is suggested by the substantially smaller proportion who perceived their local organizations as the best source of information. The fact that approximately similar proportions of left-wing and right-wing MPs cited personal friends and neighbors, also suggests that they look to the latter as possible correctives for what they have heard from party stalwarts. Finally, in view of the importance ascribed to them as "opinion leaders" in Canada,[23] it was not surprising that, as reference groups, business leaders ranked only behind the constituency parties.

In keeping with their somewhat greater reliance upon local party organizations, right-wing legislators were more inclined to accept the efficacy of those organizations exerting influence upon MPs. Thus a larger proportion of Conservatives and Social Creditors said local organizations *do* and *ought* to influence[24] their representatives in Parliament (see Table 7.8).

TABLE 7.8 LOCAL PARTY INFLUENCE ON MPS BY PARTY (percentage)

| *Attitudes toward Local Party Influence* | PARTY AFFILIATION | | |
|---|---|---|---|
| | *Left-Wing* | | *Right-Wing* |
| Do They Influence? | | | |
| No | 25 | | 13 |
| Depends | 3 | | 2 |
| Yes | 72 | | 85 |
| | | Gamma = 0.29 | |
| Should They Influence? | | | |
| No | 32 | | 13 |
| Depends | 1 | | 5 |
| Yes | 67 | | 82 |
| | | Gamma = 0.40 | |
| | ($N$ = 76) | | ($N$ = 89) |

In summary, the members of the legislative parties differed somewhat in their perceptions of the functions carried out by their local organizations. Right-wing party members tended to see their local parties as being particularly busy on the day of an election, while members of the two left-wing parties tended to see their organizations as performing pre-election day activities. Apparently, the local organizations of the right-wing parties serve as reference groups for their MPs more frequently than do the local parties of the left. Relatedly, perhaps, a larger proportion of the right-wing respondents said that constituency parties do influence MPs.

## THE COHESIVENESS OF THE PARTY IN PARLIAMENT

Many American political scientists, particularly those with liberal ideological orientations, have long admired British parliamentary parties. From Woodrow Wilson to E. E. Schattschneider, the discipline and cohesion exhibited by British parties have served as a model toward which the American parties ought to aspire.[25]

The term "cohesive" literally means sticking or acting together in one or a number of ways. Research by social psychologists has indicated that interpersonal attraction, individual motivation to succeed in group tasks, and pride in group membership are factors that affect group cohesion.[26] Newcomb, Turner, and Converse[27] suggest that structural integration, sharing, consensus, and a degree of normativness also facilitate cohesive action by a group's members.

Normativeness has been defined as the degree of power a group exerts over its members by reason of its norms.[28] According to Newcomb, *et al.*[29] two dimensions of normativeness must be taken into account—those of latitude and acceptability. Latitude refers to the fact that most rules permit some variation in the degree or manner of meeting their specifications. Acceptability refers to the degree to which specified behaviors within this range are approved or disapproved by group members. Latitude and acceptability contribute to normativeness in different ways. The degree of power that any group exerts over its members decreases with latitude if almost any behavior is acceptable; it increases with acceptability because the greater the rewards and punishments associated with certain ways of adhering to a norm, the greater the group's powers.[30]

As has been suggested, some normativeness is a requisite of cohesion. If normativeness is maximal, group members will complain that the discipline is too stringent (the rules are too strict); subsequently, group morale and cohesion are likely to suffer. However, if there is too much latitude permitted, group norms will have relatively little effect and members are likely to go their own ways rather than to act cohesively.

Previous analysis and discussion already have suggested that many of the requisites of cohesive behavior are met in a Canadian parliamentary system. For example, we have seen that a substantial proportion of the respondents early in life internalized a party preference and were exposed to party-relevant attitudes and values by members of their families. That they shared and, in fact, internalized most of these party-relevant attitudes is strongly implied by the data that show that a majority were active in local or national party organizations before their election to Parliament. As well, there was fairly broad consensus among the members on what it means to be a Liberal, Conservative, New Democrat, or Social Creditor (that is, they were able to articulate differences among the parties that largely coincided with the attitudes popularly ascribed to the parties). That this consensus was manifested in shared attitudes on policy issues also was indicated by the data. We may assume that in each legislative party, continuous member interaction *further* influenced group attitudes toward the party, its values, and its norms; in addition, although it may have varied, at least *some* interpersonal attraction must have developed from these interactions. Data will be presented that strongly suggest that a majority of the members of each legislative party also took pride in their party membership and that they were motivated to achieve party goals and to succeed in party tasks. First, it should be noted that the normativeness of Canadian legislative parties certainly is not maximal. In response to the question, "How strong is the discipline of your party in Parliament?" only 18 percent said that it was "very strong," 53 percent felt that it was "strong" or at least "strong on some issues," and 29 percent perceived party discipline as "not very strong." Reinforcing our belief that party discipline is not overly stringent was the tendency of many of the respondents to preface their replies with the statement, "If by discipline you mean are we coerced, the answer is no."

Their replies to the question, "Is a caucus decision always binding? If not, under what circumstances will it not be binding?" seemingly indicate that not only is discipline in a responsible party legislature not overly stringent, but the parties allow their members almost unlimited latitude in conforming to a caucus decision. Thus, only 25 percent of the legislators said a caucus decision *always* was binding upon individual party members; almost as large a group (18 percent) said a caucus decision *never* was binding. Another 27 percent cited individual conscience as an extenuating circumstance that permitted individuals to withhold support, while 25 percent felt that decisions were only binding when major party policies were involved. On minor issues, one could be excused *if* the other party members were openly informed that the individual could not or would not support the caucus decision. The remaining 5 percent said that a person did not have to go along with a decision that might have a deletorious effect on one's constituents or that might hurt his chances of being re-elected.

On the assumption that it is one thing to oppose one's party colleagues in a meeting closed to the public and quite another to withhold public support from the party, the MPs also were asked, "Are there any circumstances when you feel it is not necessary to vote with your party? If yes, what are they?" The responses suggest that our assumption was invalid, for 72 percent of the respondents were able to cite a variety of circumstances in which they felt that MPs need not vote with their party. We have grouped these reasons into three categories (see Table 7.9).

These data not only support William Morton's[31] claim that party ties have been loosened since the Progressive era, but also imply that a substantial amount of what economist Charles Lindblom[32] termed "partisan mutual adjustment" takes place among the members of Canadian parliamentary parties. It would seem that as a result of bargaining and negotiation between the individual and his party it is possible for the former to contract out of supporting a caucus decision, or even a public position, taken by the latter. Also, it appears that there are times when the parties will adjust their decisions out of consideration for the possible unfavorable effects these

TABLE 7.9 CIRCUMSTANCES IN WHICH IT IS NOT NECESSARY TO VOTE WITH ONE'S PARTY BY LEFT-WING AND RIGHT-WING PARTY AFFILIATION (percentage)

| | PARTY AFFILIATION | |
|---|---|---|
| *When Not Necessary to Vote*[a] | *Left-Wing* | *Right-Wing* |
| When agreement reached beforehand with party | 18 | 24 |
| When constituency would be adversely affected or constituent–legislator relation threatened | 12 | 26 |
| When individual conscience would not permit | 70 | 50 |
| | ($N$ = 59) | ($N$ = 62) |

[a] Thirty percent of the right-wing legislators and 26 percent of the left-wingers said it always was necessary to vote with one's party.

decisions may have upon individual party members. In particular, they apparently hesitate to act in ways that impinge adversely upon the personal values of party members. Thus, the members claimed that they could act independently if their consciences or adverse effects upon their constituents would not permit them to support a party decision. It is true that the respondents, when asked to cite examples of "conscience" issues, were able to articulate very few. Capital punishment, divorce, and, far less frequently, birth control were the only three issues cited. Thus conscience probably is more a *theoretical* than an *actual* reason for acting independently of party, particularly, as none of the three examples cited (to the best of our knowledge) has been the subject of a party vote when the "whip was on." Still, the fact that they felt that such independent behavior was acceptable is significant. If great latitude in conforming to a discipline norm is permitted, how then do the legislative parties achieve cohesive action?

A partial answer to this question is afforded by their responses to the question, "In general, what do you discuss in caucus?" It was possible to array the MPs along a dimension ranging from the 3 percent who said caucus performs no real function, through the 64 percent who perceived the caucus as providing an opportunity to devise *ad hoc* strategies and tactics for impending House business (that is, who speaks on what bill, when, and for how long), and the 13 percent who viewed caucus as a mechanism for facilitating a catharsis of grievances by providing a forum for their expression, to those 20 percent who perceived it as a mechanism for achieving a consensus on party programs and organization. These perceptions of the functions performed by caucus varied with the left–right party affiliations of MPs (see Table 7.10).

TABLE 7.10 PERCEPTIONS OF CAUCUS BY PARTY AFFILIATION (percentage)

| | Party Affiliation | |
|---|---|---|
| *Perceptions of Caucus* | *Left-Wing Parties* | *Right-Wing Parties* |
| Nothing discussed | 3 | 2 |
| Strategy and tactics | 79 | 52 |
| Catharsis | 5 | 19 |
| Consensus | 13 | 27 |
| | ($N$ = 76) | ($N$ = 89) |

Our interpretation of these data is that they indicate that the caucuses of both the left-wing and right-wing parties facilitate cohesive party action. On the one hand, the caucuses of the two left-wing parties contribute to structural integration because they primarily are employed to plan and coordinate the performance of individual members. A smooth and efficient performance is likely to be rewarding to the individual; it may also increase or reinforce his attraction to party colleagues.[33]

On the other hand, the caucuses of the right, although they are employed to integrate group performance, also tend to be used to vent grievances and to hammer out agreement on party policies. In their discussions, the group members are likely to express to one another attitudes and opinions they really hold. Such frank and accurate interpersonal communications, to the extent that they inhibit the development of excessive group normativeness, contribute to group cohesion.[34]

Important as the caucus is, what appear to be more fundamental reasons for cohesive action are revealed in the MPs replies to the question, "What are the advantages of going along with your party?" Only 11 percent said that there were no advantages and, presumably, they did not act cohesively. This was a somewhat smaller group than the 16 percent who indicated that they would vote against their parties in a hypothetical conflict between party and constituency. Fully 23 percent of the respondents said that they were motivated to act cohesively because it was personally advantageous to both their party and themselves. Explicit in their replies was the expectation that they would be rewarded for acting cohesively or, alternately, punished for not behaving in this way. Two typical examples of such replies were, "If one has political ambitions there certainly are advantages" and "Unless you want to be a permanent back bencher you support your party. You don't want to risk your personal future by becoming known as a malcontent and disturber of the peace."

However, a majority of the legislators (48 percent) said they were motivated by a desire to see the party achieve its goals and to maintain its viability; others (14 percent) were motivated by a concern for the continued maintenance of viability of the parliamentary system itself. Typical examples of these responses were, "It's a matter of efficiency and survival. It's like fighting a war, you can't function as a party in this system without being united." "Because it strengthens the image of the party in the eyes of the public. I believe in what the Liberal party stands for. I wouldn't have joined or stayed in the party if I didn't believe in it." "It comes down to the whole system of party government in Canada. There are none of the personal advantages your question implies. The system, being a party system, simply does not tolerate MPs who disagree publicly with their parties."[35]

Explicit in these replies are pride in party membership, highly favorable attitudes toward the party,[36] concern for the achievement of party-relevant goals, and awareness of the functional efficacy of a cohesion norm. Taken together, the factors strongly imply that the majority of Canadian MPs act in concert with their parties *because they want to.* Their adherence to a cohesion norm is voluntary, and the influence that their party is able to exert upon them stems not from fear of sanctions or hope of reward, but from willing acceptance of that influence.

Research by other scholars tends to support this interpretation. For example, Austin Ranney[37] found very few cases in which Conservative and Labor parliamentary party leaders in Great Britain were able to punish the deviant behavior of MPs by preventing their renomination. In fact, the local party organizations were as likely to exercise this kind of sanction as were the party leaders. Similarly, Leon D. Epstein[38] found that although it was possible to exercise relatively moderate sanctions (such as a temporary withdrawal of the whip from rebellious party members) it was far more difficult to curb deviant behavior by a substantial and well organized group of dissident MPs. Dowse and Smith[39] argued that the coercive power available to party leaders in the British House of Commons constituted only a partial explanation of party concord.[39]

Finally, Therese May's[40] longitudinal analysis of party discipline in the New Zealand Parliament led her to reject the notion that sanctions against potential offenders inspired cohesive behavior and, instead, to argue that the socialization of MPs to existing norms through interaction in party caucus was the single most important determinant of party discipline. She also cited pressures for conformity from local party organizations and the tendency of legislators to specialize and to become dependent as other factors motivating New Zealand MPs to act in unison with their parliamentary parties.

If, as has been argued, expectation of reward and fear of sanctions are less important determinants of cohesive party action than a willing compliance to a cohesion norm, why are the American congressional parties not more cohesive? Our suggestion is that the relative willingness of a legislator to accept such a norm, in great part, is a function of his perceived role as legislator. In a parliamentary system of the British model concerted party action is part of the behavior ascribed to the legislative position.[41] Thus, the individual legislator in such a system takes office expecting, and knowing significant others also expect, that he will maintain party unity. Continuous interaction with party colleagues reinforces these initial expectations. He learns that not only do almost all his colleagues share his expectations, but that each of them assumes that each of the others is prepared to act cohesively. This condition has been termed psychological substitutability,[42] and is a precondition for the internalization of a norm. Internalization of the cohesion norm probably is facilitated both by the member's belief that its strictures do not bind him too tightly, and by the opportunities afforded in his party caucus.

In contrast, an American Congressman expects, and knows that significant others in his role set also expect, that he *will not* be just a party hack, and that he will act independently or in the interest of constituents when such a course of action is prescribed.[43] This expectation is reinforced by subsequent interaction with colleagues in his own and the other party. That this norm is a part of the folklore of American Congressional politics requires no elucidation.

In summary, a majority of Canadian MPs said that it was neither necessary to always adhere to a decision made in a party caucus nor to always publicly support their parties. They were able to cite extenuating circumstances, principally, conscience issues. These data suggest that the discipline of Canadian parties certainly is not overly stringent and that cohesive party action is obtained by other than coercive measures. The data also indicate that the caucuses of both left-wing and right-wing parties facilitate such cohesion. The former help to ensure the kind of smooth and coordinated performances that party members are likely to find rewarding—performances that will help bind them to their parties. The latter, as they help ensure a frank exchange of opinions that the members really hold, inhibit the development of excessive normativeness and, in this respect, contribute to cohesive party action. The data further reveal that only a minority of the legislators, regardless of party, are motivated to act cohesively out of fear of sanctions being invoked against them, or in the hope of being rewarded for such behavior. The majority apparently are motivated by a concern for the attainment of party-relevant goals, and by a concern for the continued viability of both the party and parliamentary system. It was argued that party discipline in a British model parliamentary system stems from the willing acceptance of a cohesion norm. The acceptance of such a norm is a function of the role expectations of legislators; that is, they initially take office with the expectation that they will act in concert with their party. This expectation is reinforced by interactions with party colleagues and, eventually, a cohesion norm is internalized. Internalization is facilitated by party caucus and the fact that the legislators do not regard discipline as being excessively stringent.

## *SUMMARY*

Data were presented which indicated that the ideological positions of Canadian MPs, if not completely congruent with their parties' popular images, at least are shared by a substantial proportion of each party group.

Insofar as local party organizations are concerned, it would appear that the latter constitute important reference groups, as the legislators look to them for advice and for information about constituents' attitudes and opinions. In addition to performing these functions, the constituency parties also carry out a variety of electoral tasks. Their importance to the MPs may be inferred from the fact that a majority of the respondents, regardless of party, said that local parties do and *ought* to influence them.

A majority of the MPs also felt that it neither was necessary always to adhere to a caucus decision nor to vote publicly with their party colleagues. Apparently, a Canadian MP can act independently of his party if, (1) he informs his colleagues beforehand that he intends to withhold his support (2) his relations with his constituents will be jeopardized by a party vote, and (3) his conscience will not permit him to support the party on a particular issue. Assuming that these responses are valid, party discipline in the Canadian house of Commons would not appear to be overly stringent. Yet, the Canadian parliamentary parties normally are united. The reasons for this unified action are, according to a majority of the respondents, a desire to achieve party-relevant goals and a continuous concern for the maintenance of party viability. Taken together, the data presented in this chapter indicate that Canadian MPs generally act in concert with their parties because they have internalized a cohesion norm.

## Notes

1. Heinz Eulau, "The Legislator and His Party: Majority and Minority" in John Wahlke *et al.*, *The Legislative System* (New York: John Wiley & Sons, Inc., 1962), p. 343.

2. An additional 22 percent of the references to the Liberal party, despite the fact that respondents were asked to articulate differences, were that "they (Liberals) are no different from the NDP."

3. Theodore M. Newcomb, Ralph H. Turner, and Philip E. Converse, *Social Psychology* (New York: Holt, Rinehart and Winston, Inc. 1965), p. 380.

4. Angus Campbell and his colleagues state that the viewpoint termed conservative may become "that which is reluctant to destroy the existing order of relationships, whether they be laissez faire or interventionist. The liberal viewpoint sees room for improvement in the product of social and political process through change in these relationships." Campbell *et al.*, *The American Voter* (New York: John Wiley & Sons, Inc., 1960), p. 194. In our view, the ability of diverse social and economic groups to affect and take part in the making of public decisions largely has been a characteristic of democratic societies in the twentieth century. Persons with attitudes favorable toward this relatively new phenomenon may be thought of as "liberals." Conversely, those opposed may be labeled "conservative."

5. Campbell, p. 192, defines ideology as "a particularly elaborate, close-woven and far-ranging structure of attitudes . . . such that we expect an ideology to encompass context outside the political order . . . social and economic relationships and even matters of religion, education and the like." Undoubtedly, the following ideological positions of Canadian legislators encompass and have been affected by more than their party-related differences. Yet in concerning ourselves only with these differences we feel that we have focused upon the single most important determinant of their overall ideological positions. Campbell and his colleagues also have demonstrated empirically that, even at the mass level, responses to each element of American national politics are deeply affected by enduring individual party differences. Philip E. Converse has shown that party preference is particularly salient for the ideology of a political elite, as party affiliation was strongly related to the positions of congressional candidates on selected policy issues. Philip E. Converse, "The Nature of Belief Systems in Mass Publics", in David Apter (ed.), *Ideology and Discontent* (New York: The Free Press, 1964), p. 228. Herbert McClosky's findings (that Democratic and Republican party elites differed much more sharply in their ideological positions on policy issues than did their supporters in the electorate) also illustrate the importance of party affiliation for political elites. See Herbert McCloskey, Paul J. Hoffman, and Rosemary O'Hare, "Issue Conflict and Consensus among Party Leaders and Followers," *American Political Science Review,* **54** (1960), 406–427. Thus, previous research indicates that for a political elite such as we studied, party affiliation constitutes a kind of "conceptual net" for capturing, organizing, and evaluating incoming information which may be politically relevant.

6. Respondents were asked, "Since Canada is officially a biethnic and bicultural country insofar as Parliament and the courts are concerned, do you think that certain governmental practices and customs should be changed to implement this fact?"

7. Not unnaturally, such demands generated negative feedback, such as a 1962 speech by the chairman of the school board of the city of Hamilton. In it, he strongly opposed the teaching of any French in Hamilton public schools on the ground that the French should have learned English two hundred years ago.

8. For a good discussion of the 1957 national election see John Meisel (ed.), *The Canadian General Election of 1957* (Toronto: University of Toronto Press, 1962).

9. The interviewees' responses to the question were classified as "in favor,"

"pro-con" (both for and against), or "against." They were told: "As you know, we have had cases involving civil liberties in our own country. For instance, under the Padlock Act of 1957 the Quebec legislature empowered the provincial Attorney-General, whenever he felt he had adequate evidence, to padlock any house and sieze any literature without a conviction of any sort. The overt purpose of this act was to make illegal the spreading of communism in Quebec. A leading authority on Canadian constitutional law said of the act: "I know of no other equivalent attempt at thought control in the history of Canada." However, defenders of this piece of legislation have argued in favor of it on the grounds that a democracy has a right to protect itself from subversion by preventing communists from meeting together to propagate communism. What are your opinions on this issue?"

10. See *Switzman versus Elbing and Attorney-General of Quebec* in the Supreme Court, (1957), S.C.R. 285, 7 D.L.R. 2d 337, 117 Can. C.C. 129.

11. The following three questions were encapsulated in a "Welfare-State" Index with three positions—strongly favor, moderately favor, strongly oppose. "In domestic issues involving the federal Government do you favor the Government's sponsoring programs such as large-scale public works to maintain full employment, or do you think that economic problems such as unemployment ought to be left more to private individuals or provincial and local government to work out?" The choices were: (1) favor federal government activity, (2) pro–con, and (3) against activity. "Do you feel the federal Government has done too much, enough, or not enough in using federal power and funds to help solve the unemployment problem?" The choices were: (1) done too much, (2) enough, and (3) not enough. "Are you in favor of the federal Government using public funds to underwrite the cost of hospital and medical care for the people of Canada or do you favor a private plan such as those offered by insurance companies?" The choices were: (1) favor federal Government activity, (2) pro–con, and (3) opposed.

12. See V. O. Key's discussion of the innovation function ascribed to the Democratic party in the United States in V. O. Key, *Politics, Parties and Pressure Groups,* 5th ed. (New York: Thomas Y. Crowell Company, 1964), pp. 200-222.

13. See Stouffer, Guttman, Suchman, Lazarsfeld, Star, and Clausen, *Studies in Social Psychology in World War II, Vol. IV: Measurement and Prediction* (Princeton, N.J.: Princeton University Press, 1950), pp. 46-361.

14. Four Conservatives, two Liberals, and one member of the NDP did not answer these questions.

15. The actual questions were: "A person who is suspected of being a communist should not be permitted to teach in a school or college." The choices were: (1) agree, (2) pro–con, and (3) disagree. "People can follow any religion they like, but they should not be permitted to influence others in public or to be contacting a person in his home. The choices were: (1) agree, (2) pro–con, and (3) disagree. "Under our form of government every individual should take an interest in government directly, not through pressure group organizations." The choices were: (1) agree, (2) pro–con, and (3) disagree. "Labor Unions are useful but they really have too much power for the public good." The choices were: (1) agree, (2) pro–con, and (3) disagree.

16. Lewis Bowman and George R. Boynton, "Activities and Role Definitions of Grassroots Party Officials," *Journal of Politics,* **28** (1966), 121–143.

17. To date, the most ambitious has been Samuel J. Eldersveld's study of party organization in Wayne County. See Samuel J. Eldersveld, *Political Parties: A Behavioral Analysis* (Chicago, Ill.: Rand McNally & Company, 1964). See

also Peter H. Rossi and Phillips Cutright, "The Impact of Party Organization in an Industrial Setting," in Morris Janowitz (ed.), *Community Political Systems* (New York: The Free Press, 1961), pp. 81–116; Lester Seligman, "Political Recruitment and Party Structure," *American Political Science Review,* **55** (1961), 77–86; and Samuel C. Patterson, "Characteristics of Party Leaders," *Western Political Quarterly,* **16** (1963), 332–352.

18. They were asked: "What were the chief things the party organization did to help you get elected?" Only their first responses have been analyzed.

19. Unlike Bowman and Boynton, we have coded their first responses *only* on the assumption that they were the most important contributions of the organizations.

20. Assuming that their responses were not overly influenced by the traditional reluctance of candidates for elected office to discuss campaign finances, it would appear that individual campaigns largely are financed (singly or in combination) by the central offices of the national or provincial party organizations, local donors outside the formal party, or by the candidates themselves.

21. Compared with American Congressmen, Canadian MPs apparently make limited use of questionnaires and surveys to determine constituency attitudes.

22. The question was: "From whom do you think you get the most accurate information about the feelings of your constituents?"

23. See, for example, Peter Regenstrief, *The Diejenbaker Interlude: Parties and Voting in Canada* (Toronto: Longmans, 1965).

24. The two questions were: "Do you think the local party organization leaders have influence over the MPs?" and "Do you think they *should* have influence?"

25. See for example the report of the Committee on Political Parties, American Political Science Association, E. E. Schattschneider, "Toward a More Responsible Two-Party System," *American Political Science Review,* Supplement (September 1950); Stephen K. Bailey, *The Condition of Our National Political Parties* (Santa Barbara, Calif.: The Fund for the Republic, 1959); and James M. Burns, *The Deadlock of Democracy* (Englewood Cliffs, N. J.: Prentice-Hall, Inc., 1963).

26. See Kurt W. Back, "Communication in Experimentally Created Hierarchies" in L. Festinger, K. Back, S. Schachter, H. H. Kelley, and J. W. Thibaut, *Theory and Experiment in Social Communication* (Ann Arbor, Mich.: Institute for Social Research, 1950); and "Influence through Social Communication," *Journal of Abnormal Social Psychology,* **46** (1951), 190–207. See also, L. Festinger, S. Schachter, and K. W. Back, *Social Pressures in Informal Groups: A Study of Human Factors in Housing* (New York: Harper & Row, Publishers, 1950).

27. Newcomb *et al.,* pp. 383–384.

28. Newcomb *et al.,* p. 376.

29. Newcomb *et al.,* p. 376.

30. Newcomb *et al.,* pp. 375–384.

31. William Morton, *The Progressive Party in Canada,* (Toronto: University of Toronto Press, 1963).

32. Charles Lindblom, *The Intelligence of Democracy* (New York: The Free Press, 1965), pp. 3–66.

33. Newcomb *et al.,* p. 384.

34. Newcomb *et al.,* p. 384.

35. Allan Kornberg, "Caucus and Cohesion in Canadian Parliamentary Parties, *American Political Science Review,* **60** (1966), 83–92.

36. Illustrative of these highly favorable attitudes are the rather staggering functions the respondents ascribed to parties. Thus, 37 percent perceived them as maintainers of the viability of the parliamentary system; 20 percent felt they

functioned as parsimonious selectors of policy issues; 13 percent said parties provided policy alternatives to the electorate; 10 percent saw them as vehicles of social change; 11 percent said they performed a linkage function in that they made the decision-makers accessible to the public; and 4 percent felt they were socializing agents that educated the public to matters political. Only 5 percent ascribed to them such negative functions as creating cleavages within society. Interestingly, all of this latter group were members of the Social Credit party.

37. See Austin Ranney, *Pathways to Parliament* (Madison, Wis.: Univerity of Wisconsin Press, 1965), pp. 42–51 and 142–146.

38. See Leon D. Epstein, "Cohesion of British Parliamentary Parties," *American Political Science Review,* **50** (June 1956), 360–377.

39. R. E. Dowse and T. Smith, "Party Discipline in the House of Commons," *Parliamentary Affairs,* **16** (1962–1963), 159–164.

40. Therese May, "Parliamentary Discipline in New Zealand since 1954," *Political Science,* **17** No. 1 (1965), 37–54.

41. For example, in an insightful essay H. McD. Clokie, an expert on Canadaian parliamentary politics, contended that "the unity of Canadian parties was expected by the public as the *very* condition of party government of the Cabinet variety." H. McD Clokie, "The Machinery of Government" quoted in Leon D. Epstein, "A Comparative Study of Canadian Parties," *American Political Science Review,* **58** (1964), 52.

42. Newcomb *et al.,* pp. 244–245.

43. Ralph K. Huitt, "The Morse Committee Assignment Controversy: A Study on Senate Norms," *American Political Science Review,* **51** (1957), 313–330. This study affords an excellent illustration of how difficult it has been to curb the "maverick" tendencies in American Congressmen and how infrequently sanctions have been invoked by the parties to punish deviant behavior. See Lewis Froman, "The Importance of Individuality in Voting in Congress," *Journal of Politics,* **35** (1963), 324–332. Froman argues that we must be cognizant of the importance of individual predispositions if we are to understand congressional voting behavior. See also Ralph K. Huitt, "Democratic Party Leadership in the Senate," *American Political Science Review,* **55** (1961), 333–345, and Lewis Froman and Randall Ripley, "Conditions for Party Leadership: The Case of the House Democrats," *American Political Science Review,* **59** (1965), 52–63. In these two reports Huitt, Froman, and Ripley illustrate the difficulties entailed in obtaining cohesive action from a congressional party. Further, a basic criticism of American parties made by responsible party theorists such as E. E. Schattschneider and James M. Burns is that American congressional parties do not really behave like parties.

# Conclusions

This study has been concerned with legislators in a Canadian House of Commons, a parliament of the British model. We have been particularly interested in who these individuals were; the social and political environments from which they arose; the sources of their initial interest in political matters; the processes by which they were recruited for political activity, generally, and for a parliamentary position, in particular; their motives for becoming candidates and sustaining legislative careers; their goals; their representational role orientations; and their party-relevant attitudes and ideological positions.

Our underlying assumption has been that legislative behavior is role behavior, the action of the individual legislator being a series of roles taken either singly or in various combinations with significant others in his role set. It was hypothesized that legislators' roles are determined by the interaction of attitudes and expectations developed for the legislative position prior to incumbency with the values, attitudes, and perspectives subsequently developed in response to the expectations held for them by significant others in the legislative system. Insofar as the appropriate data were available an alternative hypothesis, termed "a culturalist theory," also was tested.

The extreme culturalists (almost all of whom were French Canadians) posited that the distinctive subcultural value patterns that the French-Canadian MP from Quebec has internalized, manifest themselves in generic differences in his behavior, regardless of any prescribed parliamentary norms or the expectations of significant others. Legislative behavior, rather than being a product of individual experiences both before and after incumbency in a legislative position, is determined largely by prior experiences. We should like to begin this section by commenting upon our findings concerning the motives, goals, and representational roles of French-Canadian MPs.

## FRENCH-CANADIAN LEGISLATIVE BEHAVIOR

In order to test the culturalist theory with the available data we first constructed a model French-Canadian legislator, that is, one whose background included all those characteristics that presumably manifest themselves in particular behavioral differences. When positions on a French-Canadian Cultural Index were cross-tabulated with the motives that respondents expressed for becoming candidates and sustaining parliamentary careers, and with the goals they articulated and the representational roles they took, we found no support for the culturalist thesis. However, when through the use of a multivariate analysis program we were able to control the effect of other variables and to examine the net relationship between a French cultural background and goals and representational roles, we found that these cultural characteristics were among the two or three independent variables most strongly correlated with variations in the dependent variables. Because the data did not fulfill the assumptions upon which this statistical program rested, multivariate analysis was intended to be heuristic; the results obtained neither prove nor disprove the culturalist thesis. However, the analysis does suggest that the culturalists may not have been entirely wrong, in that a French-Canadian cultural background probably does have some real impact upon legislative behavior. As other influences that impinge upon the French-Canadian MP (specifically, party affiliation) appear to affect him even more, one may speculate that French-Canadian MPs probably experience considerable role conflict during their tenure of office.

Let us consider, for example, the conflict a Social Credit MP must have experienced during the 1963 electoral campaign when, on the one hand, his party leaders outside of Quebec stated that in general they accepted the position that Canada was committed to accept American nuclear weapons while, on the other hand, his deputy-leader and fellow French Canadian, Mr. Real Caouette, stated repeatedly that he was unalterably opposed to such a commitment. Or, let us imagine how French-Canadian

Conservative MPs must have felt during that same campaign when their English-speaking party leaders (sometimes, in front of French-Canadian audiences) proudly boasted that the Conservative party was more committed to articulating French-Canadian interests than were the Liberals; they cited as evidence the fact that during their (Conservative) period in office, the menus in the parliamentary restraurants were written in both English and French! Again, French-Canadian Liberal MPs also must have been somewhat perplexed when Mr. Donald Gordon, the head of the publicly owned railroad system and an appointee of a previous Liberal administration, testified to a parliamentary committee that the reason there were virtually no French Canadians in top level positions with the railroad (despite the fact that the latter made up almost one-third of the national population) was that they were not adequately trained for such responsibilities.

These are examples of role conflict experienced when an individual is a member of different groups, both of which impinge simultaneously upon him. In the examples cited, the French-Canadian MPs being at one and the same time French Canadians and members of the Social Credit, Conservative, and Liberal parties presumably were faced with: (1) the necessity of supporting a position that generally was considered anathema in Quebec, (2) applauding a statement that was both patronizing and patently ridiculous, and (3) supporting positions that discriminated against members of their ethnic group because they were made by a party appointee. Such conflict is heightened when the individual finds himself present (as did many French-Canadian MPs) with members of both groups so that whatever he says or does is heard and observed by people who expect him to do different things. This kind of conflict, although painful, tends to be of an immediate and transitory nature.[1] More persistent, and probably pervading many more kinds of situations, is the conflict experienced when an individual has internalized the norms of two or more groups so that they impinge upon him whether or not he is observed by group members.[2] These are the kinds of role conflict that are most likely to be experienced by a French-Canadian MP by virtue of having internalized many of the norms of both his culture and party. In this sense, he is a kind of "marginal man" in the Canadian legislative system. His marginality has persisted because, although irritated and at times infuriated when the majority in his party have treated him as outside the "in-group," he has persisted in maintaining a cultural identity that is distinct from the English and English-oriented majority in his party.

From their responses to various questions during interviews and from off-the-record conversations it was apparent that the principal source of conflict for many French-Canadian MPs, particularly in the Liberal party, stemmed from their feelings that the obligations incurred seemed to outweigh the privileges derived from party membership. At times the party demanded that *because they were party members* they should support leaders and policies that were unpalatable to them as French Canadians. At other times it withheld from them, *because they were French Canadians,* rights and privileges to which they felt legitimately entitled because they were party members. In terms of obligations, they were expected to take the role of Liberals, Conservatives, and Social Creditors, but in terms of rights they were expected to take the role of French Canadians. Consequently, some complained that English-speaking colleagues refused to share important decision-making powers ("they act as if only *they* had the right to decide"), and to allocate to them enough or sufficiently powerful leadership positions ("they throw us a bone").

Not unnaturally, the French-Canadian MP at times has adapted to the conflicting expectations he faces by manifesting hostility, by rebelling, and by withdrawing from his party or from national politics. Thus, the Social Credit party during the 25th Parliament was wracked periodically by overt disagreements between Mr. Robert Thompson and his French-Canadian Deputy-Leader, Mr. Real Caouette. During the 26th Parliament, bitter disputes reportedly occurred in the Liberal caucus when party members split along ethnic lines over the alleged pathological behavior of certain French-Canadian party leaders. Former Conservative Cabinet Minister Leon Balcer and two other French-Canadian colleagues, after protesting in vain the policies of Mr. Diefenbaker, finally left the Conservative party and sat as Independents during the 26th Parliament. Mr. Caouette and eleven colleagues from Quebec eventually left the parent Social Credit party and formed the *Ralliement des Creditestes.* More serious, in that the nation as a whole has been deprived of their services, is that some of the most able French Canadians in public life today have chosen to hold office at the provincial rather than the national level.

Such adaptations to role conflict, however, are the exception rather than the rule. Generally, French-Canadian MPs accept or resign themselves to the demands of party because they share prevalent party ideological positions. Party discipline is not perceived as excessive (the party at times recognizes their claims for independent action) and, whether inspired by self-interest, a pride in party membership, the desire to achieve party-relevant goals, or out of a concern for the continued maintenance of the viability of their party and the system itself, they willingly accept a cohesion norm. Thus, although there undoubtedly are times when they feel they cannot live with their parties, French-Canadian MPs realize that over time they cannot live without them. This, in our view, accounts for the anomalous findings that French cultural characteristics, when all other variables are controlled, *are* rather strongly correlated with variations in goals and representational role orientations but *are not* so correlated when other factors are permitted to impinge upon them. At such times, cultural considerations give way to other needs, principally, the needs of the party. The fact that the chief architects of the culturalist theory (which our data suggest in great part is a stereotype) were themselves French Canadians, merely indicates that members of less-favored groups within a society over time can come to share an unfavorable image of themselves.[3]

Assuming that those speculations are grounded in empirical reality, let us consider the consequences that are likely to flow from the fact that the policy-oriented goals of a substantial proportion of the legislators, given the operation of the Canadian parliamentary system, are likely to remain unfulfilled. In so doing, we may generate answers to a third general question raised by the data—why prior experience variables generally are but weakly correlated with variations in legislators' goals and representational roles.

## POLICY-MAKING IN A PARLIAMENTARY SYSTEM

Systematic empirical studies of the political behavior of the American electorate have revealed that the degree of political interest, awareness, knowledge, and participation, as well as one's feeling that such participation is efficacious, are correlated with characteristics such as socioeconomic status, education, and occupation. Even a cursory examination of the data revealed that the majority of the respondents possessed precisely the kind of characteristics that are associated with a high level of political interest, knowledge, participation, and perceptions of political efficacy. Thus, many of the respondents recalled being interested in politics even as children; approximately one-quarter did not have to be proselytized, but generated their own political careers; almost one-half had held an elected public office before they became MPs; and over two-thirds had held an office in either their local or national party organizations. With such backgrounds one would expect that many of the respondents would have come to Parliament assuming that they would play a major role in the policy process. One also would expect that their assumption ought to have been modified by experience in the position, as policy innovation and evaluation in the Canadian House of Commons, as in all Parliaments of the British model, largely are the prerogatives of party leaders. Despite this, approximately three-quarters of the respondents articulated policy or policy-relevant goals. The fact that they did, suggested that many must be frustrated over an inability to realize their goals as policy-makers, and as a result, were also experiencing role-conflict with their parties. However, an examination of the data indicated that any conflict that policy-oriented legislators were experiencing, was more likely with their constituents than with their parties. Although some may have been frustrated, they apparently were not sufficiently exercised to aspire to other public offices or to want to discontinue their parliamentary careers.

The question we must consider now is how an average MP manages to reconcile his policy aspirations with the fact that policy-making is largely the prerogative of his party leaders. We will suggest three reasons why the back bench MP does not experience role conflict with his party although, obviously, there may be more. These reasons are more or less applicable to legislators in all parliaments of the British model.

First, the data have shown that many of the respondents were strongly attached to their parties before taking office—an attachment that is intensified by continuous interaction with party colleagues in Parliament. Thus, he is psychologically prepared to accept the normative prescriptions of his party.

Second, whether or not he helps decide it, the average MP tends to identify his party's policy preferences with his own. Fully 84 percent of the respondents said that the way an MP votes is almost always a true indication of his own policy feelings on an issue.[4] Consequently, his frustration over not participating meaningfully in party policy-making may be vitiated in part by the fact that he approves of the party's policy product.

Third, and most important in our opinion, the MP learns after he becomes an incumbent that his role as legislative party member entails not one but several relationships, and these relationships are prescribed as different. First is his relationship with the local party organization. We infer from responses to the questions on local party organization that one function of the MPs party role is to link the party organization in the electorate with the organization in the legislature. The data indicate frequent interaction between the MPs (particularly the members of the right-wing parties) and their local party organizations. The latter constituted the most important reference group in the constituency for almost one-half of the MPs, regardless of party affiliation. It seems safe to assume that local party attitudes and preferences that are tapped in this way are communicated to parliamentary party colleagues and leaders. We also may assume that these grass-roots communications at times either influence the opinions or change the positions of party leaders.[5] Such experiences likely are gratifying to those who are not leaders because they can perceive themselves as agents generating policy changes. Since the MPs undoubtedly also communicate and interpret the policy positions of the legislative parties to local organizations, and at times convince reluctant local organizations that they merit their support, the respondents are afforded an additional opportunity to identify in a gratifying way with their party's policies.

A second and closely related role would seem to be one of communicating, interpreting, and defending legislative party policies to interested groups in the constituency, and making known the attitudes of important constituency groups to party colleagues in the legislature. The likelihood that party norms ascribe both a communication and a service function (which certainly should promote good will for both the legislators and their parties) to back-bench MPs is strongly suggested by the legislators' reactions to hypothetical conflict situations involving party and constituency, and by the fact that virtually similar proportions of them articulated policy goals, focused on the nation, *but* took the delegate–servant role style. It already has been suggested that such behavior is likely to be perceived as functionally efficacious by the average MP.

The vitriolic nature of much of the debate in the Canadian House of Commons suggests a third role relationship; the task of those in Parliament who are not leaders is to publicly attack or defend policies that have been generated by party leaders.[6] As the brilliance of the defense and the quality of the criticism is less important than the fact that these people have a role, however limited, in the policy process, and because the MP lacks the staff assistance[7] required for an informed defense or criticism of public policy, debate frequently degenerates to the level of sycophantic praise or personal invective.

One might argue that these reasons, however plausible, of themselves do not explain how the back-bench MP can long be reconciled to the fact that he plays, at best, a limited role in the policy process. Given the level of his education, the prestigious occupation he has enjoyed, and his past political experience, he is not likely to be satisfied for any length of time with the roles of spear carrier and errand boy. Therefore, conflict eventually must develop between his party and himself.

We would agree with this argument but also would point out that the evidence indicates that in Canada, the average MP is not likely to remain in Parliament long enough to come into serious conflict with his party over an inability to realize policy goals. The high level of attrition characteristics of the Canadian system, although it may be disfunctional in certain respects, helps to insure that most of those who are likely to become disenchanted and frustrated with their party roles are returned to the status of ordinary citizens before that frustration becomes intense enough to threaten the viability of the responsible party system. Thus, the proportion (12 percent) of nonleaders with seven or more years of parliamentary experience was almost equal to the proportion (9 percent) who indicated that they did not want to sustain a parliamentary career. Conversely, those who manage to survive the attrition of increasingly frequent elections simply succeed to a position of leadership[8] from which they can realize their policy aspirations.

The comment on the functional efficacy of large turnover for the maintenance of a responsible party system leads us to a consideration of the third question raised by the data—why variations in individual background stemming from preparliamentary experiences generally were not related to variations in legislators' goals and representational role orientations.

## THE RELATIVE IMPORTANCE OF PREPARLIAMENTARY AND POSTPARLIAMENTARY EXPERIENCE FOR LEGISLATIVE BEHAVIOR

This study proceeded on the assumption that the behavior of a legislative elite can best be understood as a joint function of the interaction between the values, attitudes, and perspectives he brings with him from the social groups in which he matured and lived, and the norms and standards that he comes to internalize both from the elite group in which he assumes membership and from groups interacting with him in the legislative system. The data have not fully supported this assumption, as they indicated that differences in legislators' educational backgrounds alone[9] were consistently associated with variations in illustrative dependent behavior (goals and representational role orientations). It could be argued that the variables used to illustrate the impact of prelegislative experience on legislative behavior were simply poor choices and that the expected relationships would have materialized if other and more appropriate selections had been made. Although we recognize this possibility, our interpretation of the finding above is that legislative behavior in a British model parliamentary system largely is a function of attitudes and perspectives developed *after* incumbency.

This is not to say that prelegislative experiences are irrelevant. The data suggest that political experience in elected public office and in a party organization prior to incumbency are of particular importance in Canada, as individuals with those backgrounds are most likely to receive the uncontested nominations of their parties in districts in which the party is dominant. Thus, such prior experiences help determine not only who becomes an MP but, also, who is likely to achieve a position of leadership in the system. Further, a long period of political interest and activity in a party organization prior to incumbency is likely to facilitate the acceptance of norms to which the legislator subsequently is exposed. Most important, however, the individual in a society with a British model parliamentary system comes to the legislative position *expecting* to behave in concert with colleagues in the legislative party; he knows that the public also expects such behavior from him. Insofar as this culturally derived value is concerned, preparliamentary experience has a decided affect upon the subsequent behavior of a Canadian MP.

The internalization of a cohesion norm, however favorably disposed he is to it, occurs after he takes his seat in Parliament. The process by which it occurs is facilitated by the socializing experience afforded by caucus, and by the fact that party discipline is not excessively stringent. Apparently, the MP feels that the party respects his personal values, is cognizant of the peculiarities of his constituency, and therefore is willing to negotiate if he presses his claim for independent action upon it. Such claims are made only infrequently because most MPs want to act in concert with their party. For some, the desire springs wholly or in part from self interest. However, for the majority it stems from pride in party membership, shared attitudes and values, a desire to achieve party-relevant goals, and a belief that such behavior is required if the viability of the party is to be maintained.

Although he may experience considerable conflict over it, he generally is willing to accept the fact that party colleagues with cultural backgrounds different from his, or colleagues who represent constituencies in more favored regions, will at times seem to be granted more of the fruits and have to endure fewer of the burdens of party membership. Similarly, although he may become increasingly irritated, he is resigned to playing a small part in the policymaking process. He realizes that the interests of constituents sometimes will be given a lower priority than those of party or nation. His resignation to the facts of parliamentary life is made easier by the knowledge that other members of his party feel and will behave as he does.

In summary, once a cohesion norm has been internalized completely the Canadian MP, with few improvisations of his own, plays the roles ascribed to him by his party. Whether or not the quality of his performances would be improved if he were given more props and fewer directions is a subject best explored in some future study.

## Notes

1. Theodore M. Newcomb, Ralph H. Turner, and Philip E. Converse, *Social Psychology,* (New York: Holt, Rinehart and Winston, Inc., 1965) p. 405.
2. Newcomb *et al.*, p. 405.
3. M. Engel, H. E. O'Shea, M. A. Fischel, and G. M. Cummins, "An Investigation of Anti-Semetic Feelings in Two Groups of College Students: Jewish and Non-Jewish," *Journal of Social Psychology,* **48** (1958), 75–82.
4. Allan Kornberg, "Caucus and Cohesion in Canadian Parliamentary Parties," *American Political Science Review,* **60** (1966), 90.
5. A majority of the respondents, regardless of party, said that local party organizations *do and ought* to influence MPs.
6. Partial support for this assumption is offered by long-time Liberal Cabinet Minister J. W. Pickersgill who said of his party leader and Prime Minister, the late W. L. Mackenzie King, that the latter used the Liberal party caucus to explain "the whys and wherefores of Government action and suggested lines on which the Government could be supported most effectively." See J. W. Pickers-

gill, *The Mackenzie King Record* (Toronto: University of Toronto Press, 1960), p. 9.

7. It was argued that policy-oriented respondents interacted more with interest groups, and also tended to have more favorable attitudes toward them than did area-oriented legislators, because interest groups can serve as the functional equivalent of staff.

8. There was a correlation of 0.52 between interparty constituency competition and occupancy of a leadership post. See Allan Kornberg, "The Social Bases of Leadership in a Canadian House of Commons," *The Australian Journal of Politics and History,* **41** (1965), 331.

9. Thus, this analysis has provided still another example of the strength of the relationship between education and political behavior.

# Appendix I

## A NOTE ON INTERVIEWING

Canadian MPs are extremely busy men, and prevailing upon them to submit to an interview, which in many cases lasted for two hours, was an extremely difficult task. It would have been an impossible burden without the assistance of the Honorable Paul Martin (Liberal), currently the Secretary of State for External Affairs; Mr. Gordon Chown (Progressive Conservative), then Deputy-Speaker of the House of Commons; Mr. David Lewis (New Democratic party), deputy-leader of that party; and Mr. Robert Thompson (Social Credit), then national leader of his party. These gentlemen promised to alert their respective caucuses to my presence, to tell them briefly about the nature of the research, and to encourage them to support the research by agreeing to be interviewed. After the caucus announcements, appointments were sought with each individual selected in the sample. In the event that I was unable to secure an appointment for an interview, the names of those who had refused were referred to the above gentlemen with the request that they try to persuade their reluctant colleagues. That they were successful is attested to by the fact that I achieved 165 (96 percent) of the ascribed sample of 171 interviews.

It should be noted that interview appointments that had been arranged were frequently broken, almost always for legitimate reasons such as the respondent having to attend an emergency caucus, or having to see to the needs of some of the unexpected visitors from his constituency. Although I kept no accurate records, a fairly safe estimate would be that each appointment had to be rescheduled approximately three times.

The critical shortage of office space at the time posed a real problem because almost all interviews were taken in the respondents' offices, and virtually all the freshmen MPs had to share office accomodations. Although most respondents managed to have their offices cleared during an interview, there were times when the interview was taken in the presence of another MP and two interested secretaries.

A major problem faced by an interviewer is that of establishing rapport with his subjects. My impression is that I achieved better responses to questions in interviews I took during the day and early evening rather than to those I carried out in the late evening. In the latter instances, especially with older MPs, there was less initial attention to the questions, more requests to have questions repeated and, relatedly, a greater tendency on their part to become irritated with my attempts to probe for complete responses. Generally, interviewees become irritated with some of the sixteen agree–disagree items situated near the end of the instrument.

There was some difficulty in securing competent bilingual interviewers to assist in interviewing French-Canadian MPs who preferred to speak French. As the field editing was done at the end of each day, I was able to spot any French-Canadian interviews that in my view were inferior in quality. In such instances I normally returned to the respondents' offices accompanied by the interviewer, and tried to persuade them to elaborate on some of their responses or to answer questions that they had not completed previously. Not unexpectedly, this caused some irritation and led to protests about the inordinate amount of time already spent on the interview. Two Social Credit MPs even complained that the questions were "loaded." All these factors should be taken into account in evaluating the reliability of the data. My feeling is that, in general, I was successful in delineating their attitudes and perspectives, although only further study of other parliaments can satisfactorily establish this assumption.

# Appendix II

## INTERVIEW SCHEDULE FOR CANADIAN MEMBERS OF PARLIAMENT

One of the things we are most interested in is how Canadians get into public life.

1. How did you first become interested in politics?

2a. When did you first take a position in your party?

b. What was it?

3. Well how did you become a candidate for MP? Why?

4. Was there any particular person or group that encouraged you to enter politics?

5a. (If the respondent has not already mentioned this)
Had you ever held a public office before going into federal politics? Yes. No.
If yes, I would like to get the offices you have held.

| Office | Local | Provincial | When<br>from_____to_____ |
|---|---|---|---|
| 1st | | | |
| 2d | | | |

| Party Office | Local | Provincial | When from___to___ |
|---|---|---|---|
| 3d | | | |
| 4th | | | |

b. Had you ever held an office in your party? Yes. No. If yes, what and when did you hold them?

| Party Office | Local | Provincial | When from___to___ |
|---|---|---|---|
| 1st | | | |
| 2d | | | |
| 3d | | | |
| 4th | | | |
| Present | | | |

6a. Have any other members of your family or any close relative ever held a public office? Yes. No. If yes, what and when?

| Relative or Family | Local | Provincial | Federal | When from___to___ |
|---|---|---|---|---|
| 1st | | | | |
| 2d | | | | |
| 3d | | | | |
| 4th | | | | |

b. Have any family members or close relatives ever held a party office? Yes. No. If yes, what and when?

| Relative or Family | Local | Provincial | Federal | When from___to___ |
|---|---|---|---|---|
| 1st | | | | |
| 2d | | | | |
| 3d | | | | |
| 4th | | | | |

7. Did your father belong to the same party as you do? Yes. No. Liberal. Conservative. Other.
8. Would you say your father was (1) Very active in politics. (2) Quite active. (3) Not active in politics.
9. When you were growing up, were there discussions about politics in your home? Yes. No.
   If yes, would you say there was: (1) A great deal of discussion. (2) Some discussion.

10. When you were growing up, did you belong to any groups or organizations in which there were political discussions? Yes. No.

    If yes, check:

| Organization | Discussion | |
|---|---|---|
| | A great deal | Some |

11. Do you expect to run for Parliament again? Yes. No. Don't know.
12. Are there any other public offices you would like to seek sometime in the future? Yes. No. If yes, what?

    We would like to find out what the Canadian MP thinks about his job.

13. What are the most important things you want to accomplish as an MP?
14. Do you feel there are any differences between what you want to accomplish and what: (1) Your constituents want. (2) Your party wants.
15. If for some reason you had to give up being an MP next week, what would you miss most about this job?
16. Do you think there are any important differences between what you think your job is and what your constituents think?
17. What do you think your role as a representative entails?

18a. Do you feel that most of the other MPs from your province feel this way? Yes. No. If not, how do they differ?

b. Do you think that most of the MPs from other provinces feel this way? Yes. No. If not, how do they differ?

19. If you wanted to take a certain stand on an issue before the House but felt that a majority of the people in your constituency would want you to take a different stand, what would you probably do?
20. If you felt that a majority of your constituents were opposed to your party's stand on legislative issues, how would you probably vote on these issues?
21. Do you think that most of the time you know how the rank-and-file voters in your constituency feel about major issues that come before Parliament?
22. How do you make sure about the accuracy of the information about the feelings of your constituents?
23. From whom do you think you get the most accurate information about the feelings of your constituents?
24. Could you rank the following for me in terms of their usefulness in providing good advice or information? (Show Card 1.)
25. Approximately how often do you get a chance to talk to those people?

26a. Do you get much mail from your constituents? Yes. No. If Yes, how much?

b. Do your constituents communicate with you in other ways such as personal visits, telephoning, and so on? (Specify.)

27. Most legislators are called upon to perform services for their constituents, that is, contacting an administrative official, securing some information, and so on. How important a part of your job do the people of your constituency think this is?
28. Do you think they are more interested in these things or in your position on policy matters before the House?
29. How important a part of your job do *you* think constituency service should be?
30. How important a part do you think these services to constituents play in getting you re-elected?

31. Some MPs feel that their primary responsibility as a representative is to their constituency first and then to their province or to the country as a whole. Others feel differently. How do you feel about this matter?
32. Of course, constituencies will differ a good deal in terms of their economic, social, ethnic, occupational, and religious characteristics.
From this point of view, what are the important features of your district?
(Probe) What would you say is the most characteristic feature of your constituency?
33. How much do you think the people in your district know about you as a person?
34. What would you say is the most important thing the people in your district know about you?
35a. (If not yet mentioned) Do you think the people in your constituency know your church preference? Yes. No.
b. How much difference do you think this makes to them?
36a. How about the strength of the parties in your constituency. Would you describe your constituency as: (1) Very competitive. (2) Moderately competitive. (3) Not competitive.
b. Do you think this is changing any? How is that?
37. How strong would you say your party organization is? (1) Very strong. (2) Strong. (3) Not so strong. (4) Weak.
38. What would you say were the principal reasons for the election turning out as it did in your constituency last June?
39a. (If not already mentioned) How important was your party organization in determining the outcome of the election?
b. What were the chief things the party organization did to help you get elected?
40a. Aside from the party itself, what local groups would you say were important in determining the election in your constituency?
b. What were the most important things these groups did?
41. How much, would you say, the vote in your constituency was affected by national issues as opposed to local and provincial issues? (If not specified) What issues were they?
42. What percentage of the people in your constituency do you feel vote according to traditional party loyalties, that is they vote for you because you belong to your party, and your opponents because they belong to others?
43. Did you have to do much campaigning? Yes. No.
44. What were the main things you emphasized in your campaign?
45. What do you feel are the best ways of reaching the public during a campaign? (Ask about these methods if respondent does not mention them).
How much did you use television and radio? (1) A good deal. (2) Some. (3) Not very much. (4) None.
How much did you use advertisements in newspapers? (1) A good deal. (2) Some. (3) Not very much. (4) None.
How much did you use handbills, newsletters, and so forth? (1) A good deal. (2) Some. (3) Not very much. (4) None.
Did you make any use of opinion polls? (1) A good deal. (2) Some. (3) Not very much. (4) None.
How much did you rely on personal appearances, meetings, rallies, coffee parties, parades, and so forth? (1) A good deal. (2) Some. (3) Not very much. (4) None.
46. Do you feel you have to campaign differently in different parts of your constituency?

47. Did you give special attention to any groups or areas in your constituency? Yes. No. If yes, which ones?
48. Did you feel you had to play down certain aspects of your party's platform or record?
49. As you know, some people say that politics is a dirty game. How do you feel about this?
50. Without going into personalities, have you ever been really disgusted with the campaign activities of anyone in your party? Yes. No. If Yes, what type of activities were these?
51. Have you ever been really disgusted with the campaign activities of anyone in the opposition parties? Yes. No. If Yes, what type of activities were these?

As students of politics, one of the things we are most interested in is the place of parties in a legislative system.

52a. How important do you think parties are in a political system?
b. Why do you think this is so?
53. Do you think there can be too much party competition in a country? Yes. No.
(Probe) Under what circumstances?
54. How about the situation here in Canada? Would you say we have (1) too much party competition, (2) not enough party competition, (3) the proper amount of competition.
55. How strong is the discipline of your party in Parliament?
56a. How often does your party caucus during a parliamentary session?
b. Do you always attend? Yes. No.
c. In general, what do you discuss?
57a. Is a caucus decision always binding on all members? Yes. No.
b. If not, under what circumstances will it not be binding?
58. What are the two or three most important functions of a caucus?
59. Would you say that the way an MP votes is always:
(1) A true indication of his policy feelings on an issue.
(2) Almost always a true indication.
(3) Seldom an indication.
60. (If respondent was a member of the last Parliament) How often in the last two years have you abstained or voted against the majority of your party?
61a. Are there any circumstances when you feel it is not necessary to vote with your party? Yes. No.
b. If Yes, what are these?
62. What are the advantages of going along with your party?
63. Do you think there are fundamental differences among Canadian parties? Yes. No. If Yes, what?
64. Do you think the number of parties in Canada is a good thing? Why?
65a. In your opinion, what should the function of party leaders be in a legislature?
b. What would you say are the main reasons for the influence your party leaders in Parliament have over the party?
c. (If respondent is a leader or deputy-leader of a party, party whip, caucus chairman or a Cabinet Minister or parliamentary assistant, ask):
What would you say are the main reasons for the influence you, as a party leader, have over your party?
d. Do you think the local party organization leaders have influence on MPs? Yes. No.

e. Do you think they should have influence?

66. We have been told that every legislature has its unofficial rules of the game—certain things members do and certain things they must not do if they want the respect and cooperation of fellow members.
    What are some of these rules that a member must observe to hold the respect and cooperation of his fellow members?
67. I imagine that things could be made rather difficult for someone who didn't follow the rules. (If respondent agrees) Can you give me some examples of these things?
68. Do you think there are differences between the way MPs from your province perceive the rules and the way MPs from other provinces perceive them? Yes. No. What are some of these differences?
69. Do you frequently associate with MPs from other parties and provinces? Yes. No.
70. (If respondent is not a Cabinet Minister) Do you have many occasions to talk to a Cabinet Minister
    What is the occasion generally for such a talk?

We would like to get your views on certain issues. I know that some of these questions are rather complicated, but what we are interested in are the basic stands that underlie your evaluation of specific policies.

71. As you know, we have had cases involving civil rights in our own country. For instance, in the Padlock Act of 1957 the Quebec legislature empowered the provincial Attorney-General, whenever he felt he had adequate evidence, to padlock any house and seize any literature without a conviction of any sort. The overt purpose of the Act was to make illegal the spreading of communism in Quebec.
    A leading authority on Canadian constitutional law said of the Act, "I know of no other equivalent attempt at thought control in the history of Canada." However, defenders of this piece of legislation have argued in favor of it on the grounds that a democracy has a right to protect itself from subversion by preventing communists from meeting together to propagate communism.
    What are your opinions on this issue?
72. Do you think that the majority of your constituents feel about the same as you do on civil liberties issues?
73. Do you think the majority of your party feels the same way?
74. Do you think the Federal Government would be justified in setting up a civil rights commission that would interfere, if necessary, in provincial and local affairs to protect an individual's or a group's civil rights if they were being infringed upon by a provincial or local government?
75. In domestic issues involving the Federal Government, do you approve of the Federal Government sponsoring programs such as large-scale public works to maintain full employment, or do you think that economic problems such as unemployment ought to be left to private industry or provincial and local governments to work out?
76. Do you feel the Federal Government has done (1) enough, (2) too much, (3) or not enough in using federal powers and funds to help solve the un-unemployment problem. (Check)
77. Do you think that most of your constituents feel this way?
78. Are you in favor of the Federal Government using public funds to underwrite the cost of hospital and medical care for the people of Canada or do you favor a private plan such as those offered by insurance companies?

79. Do you think the majority of your constituents feel about the same way as you do about the role of the Federal Government in providing medical and hospital care?
80. Do you think the majority of your party feel the way you do?
81. In the field of foreign relations, Canada has made certain economic contributions to other countries. Would you generally favor the government expanding our program of economic aid to foreign countries, reducing it, or maintaining it about its present level? (Check)
82. Do you feel that we should help countries that are not as anti-communist as we are or should we help them only if they support the West?
83. What do you think about the Government's negotiation of the agreement to sell Canadian wheat to Communist China?
84a. Do you feel that we should expand our trade with China and other Communist countries?
b. Do you think that the majority of your constituents feel the same way about this as you do?
c. Do you think the majority of your party feel the same way as you do?
85a. Some people say that in any country there are important social and group conflicts as, for example, in South Africa between the English and the Boers. Do you think that in Canada such conflicts are a serious problem, a somewhat serious problem, or not a serious problem?
(If respondent replies Yes or that conflict is somewhat serious, ask):
b. What conflicts do you have in mind?
c. Do you think political parties help solve such conflicts or make them worse? How?
86a. How often do pressure groups contact you as an MP? Never. Occasionally. Frequently, but not every week. Often, at least once a week. (Check)
b. How do they contact you?
87. What do you think of these attempts by pressure groups to contact you as an MP?
88. Since Canada is officially a biethnic and bicultural country, insofar as Parliament and the courts are concerned, do you think that certain governmental practices and customs should be changed to implement this fact? If Yes, what changes did you have in mind?

## DEMOGRAPHIC DATA

Now just a few more questions about yourself and we'll be through.
1a. Are there any professional, civic, fraternal, or religious organizations to which you belong?
b. Are you an officer in any of these organizations?

| Organization | Member | Officer | Activity Level |
|---|---|---|---|

2a. What year were you born?
b. Where were you born?

3. Where did you spend most of the years that you were growing up, that is, was it in a city or town?
4a. Have you ever lived on a farm (if not mentioned)? Yes. No.
b. If Yes, where? (province)
c. Between what ages?
5. How many years have you lived in the constituency you represent? If not living in constituency, where?
6a. What was the highest grade of school you completed?
b. Graduate work in university? Professional degree? (law, medicine, and so forth)
7. Have you ever attended a parochial school? Yes. No. What years?
8. Have you attended any school outside your province? Yes. No. If Yes, what years?
9. What is your religious preference? (1) Catholic. (2) Protestant. (3) Jewish. (4) Other.
10. How often do you attend religious services? (1) Once a week. (2) Twice a month. (3) Once a month. (4) A few times a year or less. (5) Never.
11. What was the original national background of your family on your father's side?
12. Was your father born in Canada? Yes. No.
13. What was your father's usual occupation while you were growing up (be specific)?
14. What is your own primary occupation (aside from being an MP)?
15. Was this your occupation when you entered politics? Yes. No. If not, what?

Thank you for your time and cooperation!

CARD I

Editorial opinions and letters to the editor
Party leaders and workers in your district
Business leaders
Union leaders
Ministers or religious officials
Leaders of ethnic groups
Personal friends and neighbors
Friends in Parliament
Others (specify)

CARD II

1. A person who is suspected of being a Communist should not be permitted to teach in a school or college. Agree. Tend to agree. Tend to disagree. Disagree.
2. A person who has been duly elected by a constituency should be permitted to hold a legislative seat even if he is an avowed Communist. Agree. Tend to agree. Tend to disagree. Disagree.

3. If the party takes a stand on an issue, a member should vote with it even if it costs him some support in his district. Agree. Tend to agree. Tend to disagree. Disagree.
4. Business enterprise can continue to give us our high standard of living only if it remains largely free from government regulation. Agree. Tend to agree. Tend to disagree. Disagree.
5. No avowed atheist should be allowed to join a political party. Agree. Tend to agree. Tend to disagree. Disagree.
6. One should go along with a party's leaders or the party will disintegrate. Agree. Tend to agree. Tend to disagree. Disagree.
7. A democracy has a right to protect itself by legally preventing subversive groups from forming parties and trying to get elected. Agree. Tend to agree. Tend to disagree. Disagree.
8. Foreign companies that operate within our country should be directed by Canadian businessmen and staffed by Canadian workers. Agree. Tend to agree. Tend of disagree. Disagree.
9. People can follow any religion they like but they should not be permitted to influence others either in public or to be contacting a person in his home. Agree. Tend to agree. Tend to disagree. Disagree.
10. If democracy requires an informed electorate, then only informed people should be allowed to vote. Agree. Tend to agree. Tend to disagree. Disagree.
11. The best interests of the people would be served if legislators were elected without party labels. Agree. Tend to agree. Tend to disagree. Disagree.
12. Under our form of government every individual should take an interest in government directly, not through pressure group organization. Agree. Tend to agree. Tend to disagree. Disagree.
13. The most important thing for the survival of a society is to have strong leaders whom the people respect. Agree. Tend to agree. Tend to disagree. Disagree.
14. The only way to balance the power of big business today is to have a government of strong men to deal with them. Agree. Tend to agree. Tend to disagree. Disagree.
15. Labor unions are useful, but they really do have too much power for the public good. Agree. Tend to agree. Tend to disagree. Disagree.
16. Strong local and provincial governments are able to handle any problem that comes up without Ottawa's help. Agree. Tend to agree. Tend to disagree. Disagree.

*To the Interviewer:* Please include in your write-up a description of anything about the interview or the respondent that would increase my understanding of the answers.

# Author Index

# General Index